Anabaptists, Hutterites and Habans in Austria

Anabaptist Museum Niedersulz

museumsdorf**niedersulz**

Reinhold Eichinger
Josef F. Enzenberger

VTR

Publications

KULTUR NIEDERÖSTERREICH N

ISBN 978-3-941750-28-9

© 2012

VTR Publications
Gogolstr. 33, 90475 Nürnberg, Germany
http://www.vtr-online.com, info@vtr-online.com

Cover design: Jasmin Kucharz, Vienna
Translation: Eric Lundquist, Vienna
Printed by Lightning Source

Contents

Room C:
Daily Life and Cultural Activities, Language, and Artisanry of the Anabaptists 67

Rooms D + E:
Path of Suffering and Persecution –
Above All in the Region of Today's Lower Austria.................. 91

Room F:
Subsequent Groups and Spiritual Heritage
of the Anabaptist Movement –
Hutterites and Free Churches Today 119

Around the Anabaptist Museum Outside Grounds 133

View of the Anabaptist Museum in Niedersulz

Preface

The average Austrian knows very little about the Anabaptist movement. That's amazing, given the convincing power of those involved in this arm of the Reformation, whose cities and towns in modern Austria challenge us to find them again.

Only lately has local research begun to uncover this movement for the Austrian people. In the Weinviertel of Lower Austria, the Anabaptists have left their rich legacy, waiting to be rediscovered.

The establishment of this Anabaptist museum is unique in Austria. We are happy to make this history available to a wider audience.

Reinhold Eichinger
Founder: Museum of Anabaptist History in Niedersulz

Dear Visitor,

The Hutterite-Anabaptist Museum in the Museumsdorf in Niedersulz welcomes you!

This museum guide is designed to help you find your way through the museum. It includes almost all of the text you will find on display, including the names and descriptions of many artifacts included in the exhibition. This is intended to enable you to look into the subject of the Anabaptists more deeply after your visit.

The rooms are organized clockwise and are labeled from **A** to **F**.

Room A explains the basic term "Anabaptist" and describes the house in which you stand, which naturally contains the exhibition you are seeing.

Room B displays the differing parts of the Protestant Reformation, their most important representatives, and those who paved the way for them during the Middle Ages. At the same time you will get to know various people of the Anabaptist movement including their beliefs and the centers of their activity in Lower Austria, Moravia, and Slovakia, as well as important events of which they were a part.

Room C offers insight into the daily life of the Hutterites of the 16th and 17th centuries and their cultural activities.

Rooms D and E is dedicated to the painful history of the persecution of the Anabaptists.

Room F closes the exhibition with various groups of current Anabaptists and those like-minded.

Here you will meet an exciting but lesser known piece of our history!

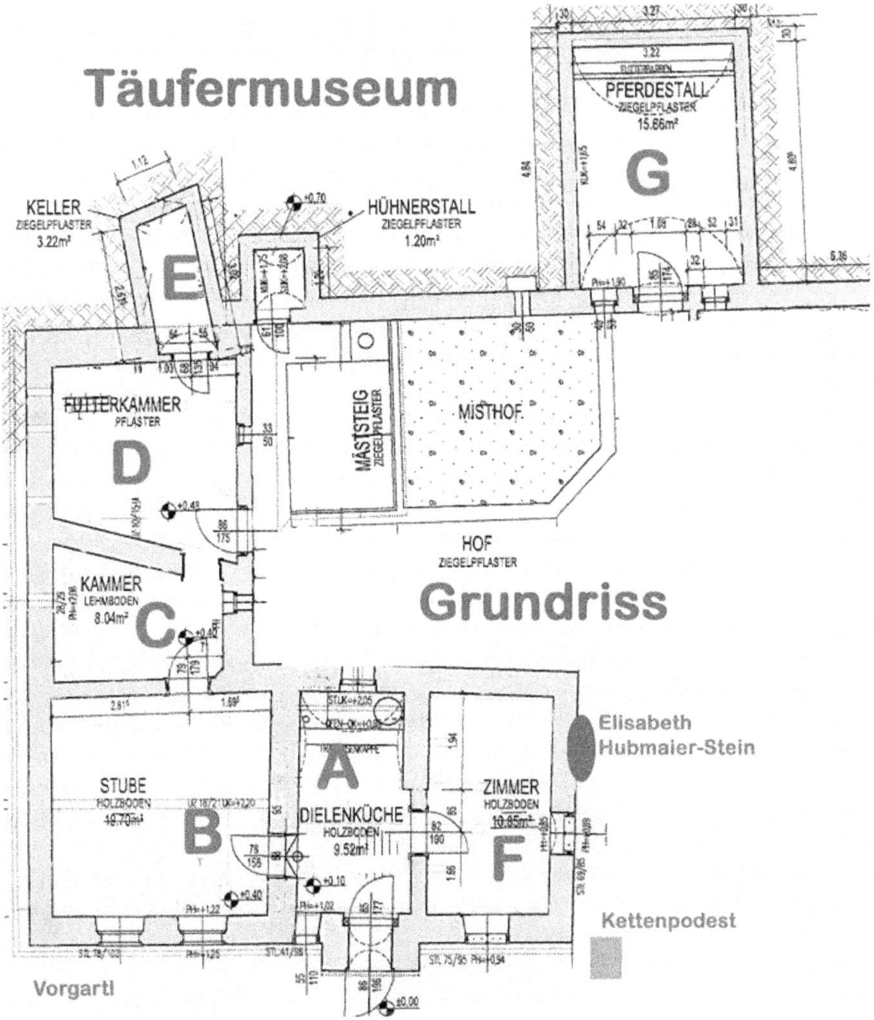

Täufermuseum

Grundriss

KELLER
ZIEGELPFLASTER
3.22m²

E

+0.70

HÜHNERSTALL
ZIEGELPFLASTER
1.20m²

PFERDESTALL
ZIEGELPFLASTER
15.86m²

G

FUTTERKAMMER
PFLASTER

D

+0.43

MÄSTSTEIG
ZIEGELPFLASTER

MISTHOF.

HOF
ZIEGELPFLASTER

KAMMER
LEHMBODEN
8.04m²

C

+0.43

STUBE
HOLZBODEN
18.70m²

B

A

DIELENKÜCHE
HOLZBODEN
9.52m²

ZIMMER
HOLZBODEN
10.85m²

F

Elisabeth
Hubmaier-Stein

Kettenpodest

+0.40

+0.10

±0.00

Vorgartl

The Small House from Wilfersdorf

This Kleinhäuslerhaus (house of a class of society that lived in small houses) from Wilfersdorf was able to be saved before its demise and now houses this Anabaptist museum. Professor Josef Geissler completed its [re-]construction in 2007 with the support of a few helpers. Even volunteers from a Christian church in Texas offered their vacation time for this project!

This house is an example of a typical L-shaped building from the Wine District of Lower Austria which resembles a "Zwerchhof" type of structure.

This house was a "Zuleuthstübl" from 1600 to 1774 and then became a "Kleinhäusel", or small house. Until 1988 this house was the home of farmers who produced their own goods, stored their own supplies, and kept a horse which contributed to the work in the fields (see the horse stall in the courtyard behind the house).

Some Anabaptist families lived in similar houses, for example, in the Steinzeile street in Nikolsburg (Mikulov).

Courtyard view of the Kleinhäuslerhaus from Wilfersdorf

Room A

Basics about the Anabaptists

Terms, Chronology and Extent

Anabaptist – Hutterites – Habans:
Ever Heard of Them?

They lived in our streets,
But were burned to ashes
and driven away.
The Anabaptist movement was all over Austria.

Their traces span five centuries
of moving history
from the farmlands of Lower Austria
to the prairies of North America!!

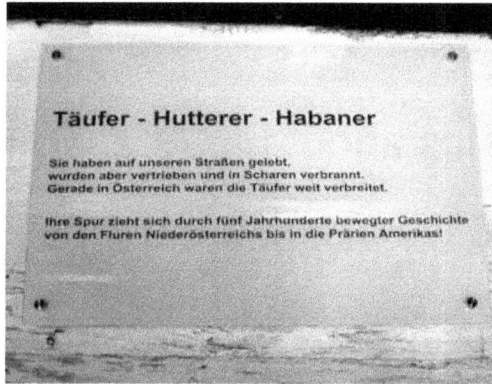

Sign over the entrance of the Anabaptist museum

The Anabaptist Movement – Basic Terms

The Anabaptist movement, a diverse phenomenon during the Reformation, spread like wildfire through Europe, in which today's Austria played an important part.

This museum displays the development of this history beginning 500 years ago.

The Anabaptists baptized only born-again Christians as a sign of their faith in Jesus Christ.

Because they had already been baptized as babies, they were taunted with the name "Re-baptizers" or "Anabaptists."

These terms emphasized their role in living out a freedom of faith and freedom of conscience.

An important group of the Austrian Anabaptist movement was the Hutterites, who lived for nearly 100 years in southern Moravia and the northern Weinviertel north of Vienna, and originated in Tyrol.

Later they were called "Habans" after they were re-catholicized. They were known for their artistic Ceramics.

Most of the Free Churches we know today stem from this 16th century Anabaptist movement. Today they make up 1/3 of all Christians worldwide.

Who Were the Anabaptists, Disparaged as "Rebaptizers"?

☞ They lived according to the Bible,
even through persecution or execution.

☞ They lived withdrawn from the rest of society,
but had a great cultural influence on it.

☞ They were diligent and industrious,
yet time and again lost all their possessions.

☞ They were ready to die for their faith,
and yet they have survived until the 21st century.

☞ They were radical in their religious views,
but also radically loved their enemies.

Who were these Christians of the 16th Century?

**Were they religious supermen –
or only people with weaknesses and limits?**

Die Täuferbewegung - ein vielschichtiges Phänomen der Reformationszeit - erfasste Europa wie einen Flächenbrand innerhalb kurzer Zeit.

Das heutige Österreich spielte dabei eine besondere Rolle!

Die Täufer vollzogen die Taufe nur an wiedergeborenen Christen als Zeichen der Bereitschaft zur konsequenten Jesus-Nachfolge.

Weil sie aber bereits als Kinder getauft worden waren, verspottete man sie als **Wiedertäufer.**

Auch als **Anabaptisten** bezeichnet, waren sie in der Betonung der Freiheit in der Glaubenswahl Vorreiter der Glaubens- und Gewissensfreiheit.

Ein wichtiger Zweig der österreichischen Täuferbewegung waren die **Hutterer**, die für fast 100 Jahre in Südmähren und im nördlichen Weinviertel gelebt haben. Viele von ihnen stammen aus Tirol.

Täuferbewegung

Der Darstellung dieser Entwicklung über ein halbes Jahrtausend ist dieses Museum gewidmet.

Aus der Täuferbewegung des 16. Jhdts. leiten sich die meisten **Freikirchen** der Gegenwart - trotz unterschiedlicher Bezeichnung - ab. Sie machen heute weltweit ein Drittel der gesamten Christenheit aus.

Später hat man jene auch als **Habaner** bezeichnet, die rekatholisiert worden waren. Bekannt geworden sind sie vor allem durch ihre kunstvollen Keramikarbeiten.

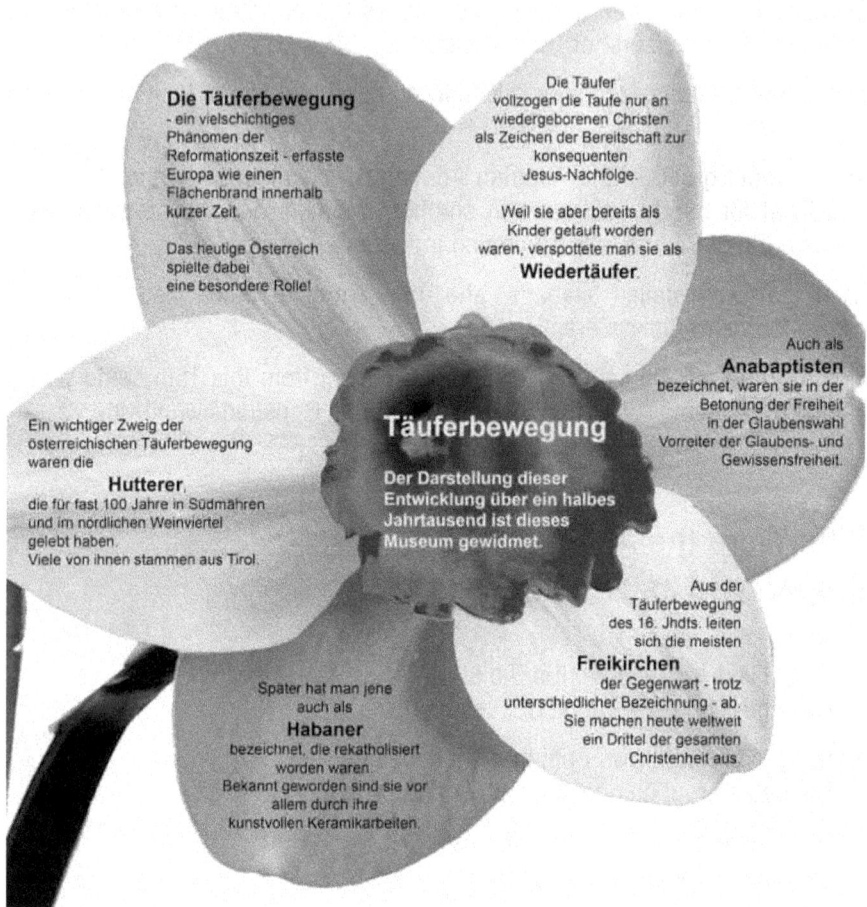

This picture is in the entry of the museum and serves as a glossary of the most important terms of the Anabaptist movement in Austria.

This museum is dedicated to the depiction of this movement's development over a half-millennium.

The Anabaptist Movement

Die "Täuferbewegung" – a multi-faceted movement from the Protestant Reformation – overwhelmed Europe like a wildfire in a short period of time.

Die Täufer (Anabaptists): The Anabaptists baptized only born-again Christians as a symbol of their willingness to consistently follow Jesus Christ.

Wiedertäufer (Re-baptisers): Because they had already been baptized as children, they were mocked as "re-baptisers".

Anabaptisten (Anabaptists): Also known as Anabaptists (re-baptisers), they were some of the first to emphasize freedom of faith and conscience.

Freikirchen (Free Churches): Most independent, evangelical churches of today, despite their various names, find their roots in the Anabaptist movement of the 16th century. Together they comprise one-third of all Christians worldwide.

Habaner (Habans): Some were later known as Habans. Most of them recatholicized. They are most well known for their artistic ceramics.

Hutterer (Hutterites): An important group of the Austrian Anabaptist movement, which lived for nearly 100 years in southern Moravia and in the northern Wine District. Many of them originated in Tyrol.

The Anabaptists in Lower Austria –
Persecution, Death ... and Loving Others

Lecture given at the Inauguration of the Anabaptist Museum
on October 5, 2009 Astrid von Schlachta, University of Innsbruck

The Reformation was not just a "media revolution," but paved the way for other confessions, making the spectrum of Christianity broader than the "old" church with their differing perceptions of the Christian faith. One of those groups during the throes of the Reformation was the Anabaptists, gaining followers in spite of their opposition to the religious-political "establishment", opposing the Roman Catholic Church with their values and standards. "Scripture alone, grace alone, faith alone" – these were the principles the reformers preached – which became part and parcel of their doctrinal statements, though the Anabaptists took them a few steps further than most. They practiced, for example, believer's baptism (adult baptism), avoided taking oaths, established local churches separate from the established church parishes and secular authorities, and rejected military service including paying taxes that funded war. The common sharing of material goods was the distinguishing characteristic of the Anabaptists.

The explosive force behind this early modern society was the refusal to take oaths, since this was the common way regional authorities secured the loyalty of their subjects. Although the Anabaptists were in no way "radical" in relation to governing authorities (recognizing and allowing for their keeping of the peace), their simple refusal to swear an oath of allegiance to local authorities or to bear arms was enough to signal rebellion, revolt, and insurgency; this is what finally led to serious opposition to their movement.

A closer look at the Anabaptists of Lower Austria and their neighbors in Moravia reveals a multifaceted, heterogeneous movement. It was affected by influences from the west and the north, including that of Hans Hut, an Anabaptist from the German region of Thuringia (located in the center of modern Germany) who had a close connection with the ideas of Thomas Müntzer. He fought with Müntzer in the Peasant's War of 1525. A hallmark of his theology was the "Gospel of All Creatures" – a specific interpretation of Romans 1:19. "Because that which may be known of God is manifest in them; for God hath shewed it unto them." Hut also had made the "mystical" ideas from Thomas Müntzer his own; he considered the end of the world to be imminent and the second coming of Christ to be near. Hans Hut became an important Anabaptist missionary, whose legacy can be found in various regions of Lower Austria. For example, it is well-known that he spent time in the Kärtnerstrasse of Vienna. His heated conversations in 1526 with Balthasar Hubmaier in Nikolsburg, Moravia, were a pinnacle of Anabaptist activity in that city as well.

Historically relevant locations
regarding Anabaptist history in Vienna in the early modern era.

Having noted Hut's conflicts with others, we come to the second important protagonist of Lower Austrian-Moravian Anabaptism, Balthasar Hubmaier. His influence helps explain the development of the early Anabaptists. Like Wilhelm Reublin and Konrad Grebel who also later became Anabaptists, Hubmaier, too, was involved in the Peasant War of 1525. One point of conflict was the peasants' refusal to give ten percent of their wages to the authorities. Political-economic radicalism was strong at play. After their defeat, these peasants changed some of their ethical standards, deciding it admissible to pay certain taxes to authorities. Hubmaier, too, lost his political radicalism.

Beginning in 1524 the lords of Liechtenstein brought the Reformation to their lands and surrounding territories. They opened their city gates to Anabaptist refugees of which Hubmaier was also a part. In Nikolsburg he had his greatest experience with Anabaptist thought. Hubmaier, who was a regular preacher in the city, demanded objective listening to the biblical text. The New Testament and the oldest testimony of the early church taught that only those who have heard the Gospel, have believed it, and have publicly confessed it, are eligible for baptism, criteria that infants and small children can't fulfill.

The political theology of Hubmaier was in no way radical as the following quote demonstrates: "The Holy Scripture alone is the judge of what I teach, whose God has given the sword to protect the devout and to punish evil do-ers." Thus, Hubmaier was able to win Leonhard von Liechtenstein and his nephew Hans to his viewpoint.

Not long after this, however, the political climate changed. With the death of the Bohemian-Hungarian King Ludwig II Jagiello at the Battle of Mohács in 1526, the territories of the Bohemian crown fell into the hands of the Haps-burgs. In the summer of the following year, the lords of Liechtenstein were forced to deliver Hubmaier and his wife to Vienna. For Hubmaier, this meant death by being burned at the stake, and for his wife by drowning. Neverthe-less, Hubmaier's legacy lived on, and his theological writings formed the foundation of many Anabaptist communities.

A look at the different parts of the Anabaptist puzzle makes it clear that they were well-networked and multinational in composition. Countless individuals blanketed the eastern and western regions of the Habsburgs' lands and led difficult lives. One of these, an Anabaptist preacher, was Wolfgang Brandhuber. Traces of his life can be found in Linz, Wels, and Mauthausen and finally in Rattenberg, Tyrol. His ideas show that he was a close forerunner of the Hutter-ites, being that in his letters he postulates early concepts of shared wealth and communal living. In an Anabaptist household, which in that time included ser-vants, maidservants, and laborers, all could share everything in common. The Anabaptist preachers Leonhard Schiemer and Hans Schlaffer too were included among traveling preachers; coming from the eastern side of the Habsburgs' lands they met their respective deaths at Rattenberg and at Schwaz.

Anabaptist history presents itself as a story of beginnings and renewal which summarily led to persecution and expulsion. This leads us to ask why such dark shadows fell on these waves of reform, that is, who did the persecuting and why? The answer is multi-faceted and in no way easy to explain. Gener-ally speaking, this persecution was the interaction of secular and religious authorities. Religion and politics in early modernity cannot be separated. The two constituted one thing which makes it difficult to name one or the other the scapegoat. Thus remains the question of "why?" Was baptism then seen as the danger?

When looking at historical sources, it is apparent that the Anabaptists were usually asked about their views regarding authority. Among other things, their view of oath-taking reveals their convictions. They refused to take oaths of allegiance to governing authorities, which limited the power of those governors. Anabaptists assume that all authority is put in place by God, so that good is protected and evil is punished; however, like the Lutherans, they held up a stop sign declaring that the authority of government ends when the conscience of the people is attacked.

Although Anabaptist history has been shaped by persecution and death, the "other side" of persecution should not be forgotten. The following statement is perhaps unexpected: the Anabaptists weren't as persecuted as they could have been. Although this seems to trivialize the high number of martyrs including numerous burnings at the stake, one must take into account the spirit of those times, that governors were under increasing pressure to justify their actions – they were indeed moving into early modern culture. It's true that Anabaptists were harshly condemned through decrees, the death penalty, prison sentences, and merciless persecution, but this is just one side of the story. It's also true that they were aided by non-Anabaptist resistance, quiet tolerance, and protection including being aided in hiding and emigration.

Historical sources verify that local authorities did not always fully carry out the demands of regional governments. Members of local authorities, such as city councils and judges, along with sworn witnesses in court proceedings, made up their own form of "resistance" in order to express their discontent with the doings of the respective regional authority. For example, sworn witnesses sometimes refused to testify against Anabaptists. Even provincial governors like Hans Ungnad von Sonneck, the governor of Styria who was also a Lutheran, tried to have as little to do with Anabaptists as possible. In March 1528, Ferdinand I overturned a light sentence by the city judge of Steyr against Anabaptists. It was only by order of the regional magistrate that Anabaptists were executed. The road from Tyrol to Moravia, which many Anabaptists took [to escape persecution], was lined with sympathetic and helpful people who offered travelers shelter and food. Early modern governance thus had sand in its gears, and was unable to persecute Anabaptists like it could have otherwise. The gap between what the law stated and what was enforced – an old comparison – is seen in many ways in Anabaptist history.

The history of the Anabaptists in Lower Austria would only be half told if the neighboring region of Southern Moravia was excluded. The religious landscape of Moravia was multi-faceted in the early 16th century – one of the largest and enduring groups was the Hutterites. The southeast section of Bohemia, the margraviate of Moravia, meant for them the possibility to live out their apostolic way of life with clarity and conviction.

Not only that, but Moravia meant an escape from persecution and distress. At that time in Moravia there were descendants of the Hussite Reformation of the 15th century called Utraquists (of the Lutheran or Reformed confession) who proved to be accepting of new settlers. Many regions of the area were not inhabited after the plague came through in the 15th century, so that many land owners welcomed newcomers who could live in depopulated tracts of land and make them again inhabitable. The immigrants who streamed through Moravia's open door soon brought about an economic upswing and money flowed into the pockets of those landowners.

Hutterite family in front of a community settlement.
Front picture of an inflammatory pamphlet by Christoph Erhard, printed in 1589 by Adam Berg, Munich

The Anabaptists again profited from this "reciprocal business" by living under tolerance and later by gaining respect as a society without persecution and threat of death.

Even still in November 1581 the rector of the Jesuit novitiate in Brunn described in a letter to Rome the situation in Moravia with these words: "Only a small number of meaningless people still confess the catholic religion. Almost all of the nobility are caught up in every kind of false teaching. I have been all around, having travelled through nearly all of Germany, and have never found such a place on earth where so many sects and false teachings can be found like here. Moravia is, so to speak, a reservoir of every possible heresy on the earth."

But in the first half of the 16th century, Moravia did not always show its positive side, though after two small waves of persecution the Hutterites were allowed to build their own communities into prosperous and recognized enclaves in the region. For example, a government order was given in 1570 which set a tax on the Anabaptists, intended to make them normal, tax-paying residents of the land. The Hutterites' contacts with the nobility grew including contact with Cardinal Franz von Dietrichstein, who was responsible for carrying out the expulsion of non-Catholic subjects from Moravia. The relationship with Dietrichstein reflected a double-mindedness, which showed itself over and over, that even good, personal contact and protection couldn't guard against persecution and expulsion in the end.

The Hutterite Anabaptists lived out their own ideals. Thus it is necessary to be careful when looking back at their history not to idealize them, even though their own "Hutterite Chronicles" tends to paint unrealistic pictures of them. Their communities of shared wealth soon became the pitfall of the Hutterites. The economic upswing they experienced in southern Moravia became the biggest enemy of their communal way of life and group ownership of property. Prosperity wet their appetite for luxury and private ownership of property.

The growing number of Brethren communities in the second half of the 16th century required the Hutterites to create official, administrative structures and institutions in order to properly manage their communities. The effects of these improvements brought about a greater level of efficiency and were so positive in nature, that the character of the original movement itself was diminished. Hierarchization and institutionalization are keywords that describe this process. This process took a loosely organized "movement" and turned it into a church with structures similar to the state church. Nevertheless the groundwork was laid for stable, long-lasting communities of people who would be able to live together. This level of organization developed early on, helping these Anabaptists to survive later crises when their communities were on the brink of ruin, since practices and policies were thought through and written out, providing time and again the foundation for renewed life together.

Near the town of Niedersulz is a place which is of great historical significance for the Anabaptist/Hutterite movement, the Castle of Falkenstein. In 1539 the Hutterites from communities in and around nearby Steinabrunn were incarcerated before they were expelled to Triest and enslaved on galley ships. The dramatic fate of those prisoners and their journey to Triest is just as gripping as that of those left behind, mostly women and children. Their communities had to survive, meaning that the women had to do nearly every kind of work. Shortly after these events, the Hutterite elder Hans Amon wrote a letter to those remaining in Steinabrunn. "You my Martl, Oswaldin, you my Maierin, and Ursula our housekeeper, and all you dear sisters in the kitchen, with the livestock and all the others too numerous to mention by name, I entrust you to the will of our most loving and dear Father and Lord." And Amon writes further: "May He be your comfort, protection, shield, and shelter in Christ Jesus our Savior. May he give you all the heart of a man, a steadfast mind, a sturdy faith, a happy and invincible hope and fill you with all long-suffering, which may help you be fully patient with His will and able to accept discipline from the bottom of your heart. The Lord will be with you all, through flame and flood, and in every temptation bring about a gracious end. All of this shall be your supply from God in heaven."

Sources:

Goertz, Hans-Jürgen, Die Täufer, München 1980.

Hrubý, Frantisek, Die Wiedertäufer in Mähren, Sonderdruck aus dem Archiv für Reformationsgeschichte 30-32, Leipzig 1935.

Mecenseffy, Grete, Ursprünge und Strömungen des Täufertums in Österreich, in: Mitteilungen des Oberösterreichischen Landesarchivs 14, 1984, 77-94.

Packull, Werner O., Die Hutterer. Frühes Täufertum in der Schweiz, Tirol und Mähren (Schlern-Schriften, 312) Innsbruck 2000.

John D. Roth / James M. Stayser (Hgg.), A Companion to Anabaptism and Spiritualism, 1521-1700 (Brill's Companions to the Christian Tradition, 6), Leiden/Boston 2007.

von Schlachta, Astrid, Die Hutterer zwischen Tirol und Amerika. Eine Reise durch die Jahrhunderte, Innsbruck 2006.

Westin, Gunnar / Bergsten, Torsten (Hgg.), Balthasar Hubmaier. Schriften (Quellen und Forschungen zur Reformationsgeschichte, 29), Gütersloh 1962.

Timeline of the Anabaptist Movement

Beginnings of the Movement

1489   Zwingli enrolls at the University of Vienna.

1517   Luther's 95 Theses nailed on the church door at Wittenberg, the beginning of the Reformation.

1521   Luther at the Diet of Worms.

1524   Initial discussions of Zwingli with future Anabaptists Konrad Grebel and Felix Manz;

Contact established between the radical group of Grebel and Manz with Thomas Münzer.

Balthasar Hubmaier's alignment with the Anabaptist's radical rejection of infant baptism.

1525   First adult baptisms in Zurich. Release of Zwingli's publication against the Anabaptists.

1526   Hubmarier's arrival of Hubmaiers in Nikolsburg and building of an "Anabaptist community".

1527   The first Anabaptist articles of faith: the 7 "Schleitheimer" Articles Disputation at Schloss Nikolsburg between Balthasar Hubmaier and Hans Hut. Founding of countless Anabaptist communities throughout the whole area of the Habsburgs.

1528   Designation of "Staff Carrier" (against any form of violence) from Nikolsburg and the settling of Anabaptists at Austerlitz. March 10th: Dr. Balthasar Hubmaier is burned at the stake in Vienna.

1529   2nd Speyr Diet: mandate against the Anabaptists. Jakob Hutter flees from Tyrol to Austerlitz, which becomes the focal point of the Anabaptist movement in the next few years.

1533   Beginning of community ownership of property under Hutter's leadership in Auspitz.

1534 to 1535: Beginning of radical Anabaptist government in Münster.

1534 to 1535: **Beginning of the first major wave of persecution**. The arrest of several Anabaptists in Hohenwarth am Manhartsberg and imprisonment at Eggenburg.

1536   February 25th: Jakob Hutter is burned at the stake in Innsbruck.

1537   Hans von Fünfkirchen allows the creation of a Brethren community in Steinebrunn.

1539   Attack on the Brethren community in Steinebrunn and sentencing to work on slave ships.

1546 to 1554: **Second major wave of persecution**

1555   Religious Peace of Augsburg ("Cuius regio, eius religio").

c. 1565-1589 Apex of the Hutterites: in Moravia 57 Brethren communities with an average of 400 people in approximately 25 areas.

Timeline of the Counter-Reformation

Counter-Reformation and Decline

1599 Dietrich Franz von Stein, opponent of the Anabaptists, becomes cardinal and bishop of Olomouc

1620 to 1622: Battle of White Mountain; Third major wave of persecution

1622 Expulsion of radical Hutterites from Moravia, escape to West Hungary (now Slovakia, Burgenland), construction of Brethren communities at Kittsee and Mattersburg

1685 Gradual decline of western Anabaptist communities, dissolution of communal ownership of property in Velke Levare / Großschützen

1685 Hutterites in Transylvania, dissolution of communal property in Alwinz

1725 Hutterite communities east of the March River (today Slovakia) become heavily crowded by Jesuits

1733 Imperial mandate that infants may only be baptized by Catholic priests

1755 Queen Maria Theresa deports large groups of "Krypto" Protestants from Carinthia to Transylvania under dishonorable circumstances; Some join the Hutterites.

       There is a spiritual revival in the community

1767 Hutterites from Transylvania flee from Joseph Kuhr in Walachia

1770 This group finds refuge in Wischenky (Ukraine). They receive privileges such as religious freedom and military service exemption.

1781 October 10th: the Edict of Tolerance of Josef II ensures Lutheran, Calvinist and Orthodox religious freedom – but not for the Anabaptists!

The Anabaptist movement didn't survive the Counter Reformation. Since the 19th century modern Austria has not had any Anabaptist communities.

Timeline of Anabaptist Free Churches of the Present

1847   October 28th: The Baptist missionary F. Oncken baptized a husband and wife named Marschall in the ship canal of Wiener Neustadt.

1861   April 11th: The Edict of Tolerance, issued by Emporer Franz Joseph, made Catholics and Protestants legally equal.

1874   Beginning of emigration to North America due to the imposition of military service. 18,000 Mennonites and 1,250 Hutterites move via Hamburg.

1883   The Austrian scientist Dr. Josef von Beck publishes in Vienna the book "History Books of the Anabaptists in Austria-Hungary."

1923   Viennese literary historian Rudolf Wolkan writes a work on the songs of the Anabaptists.

1998   Baptism-minded free churches are allowed for the first time in Austria to be officially registered as religious organizations. A legal equality with other Churches has not yet been granted.

2007   In Austria, no more Hutterite communities exist.
        World-wide there are about 50,000 Hutterites in 480 groups

2008   More than 600 million Christians belong to those who are Baptism-minded. This grouping includes one-third of global Christianity.

Austria-wide, the number of Baptism-oriented congregations (free churches) has continually risen since 1960.

There are over 250 individual churches in Austria. Many of them belong to an association of Evangelical churches.

These churches are still waiting for a legal equality with the State Churches.

After half a millennium of expulsion, persecution, dispossession, prison, torture, and massive eradication attempts, the Anabaptists (now the evangelical, free churches) are still not recognized legally as a church or religious society.

The evangelical free churches are among
the fastest growing churches in Austria,
but legally do not have an equal footing
with other churches.

Baptisizing Free Churches of the Present

Hutterite Women's Clothing (exhibition description)

Hutterite woman's dress from a "Lehrleut" community in Montana, USA, consisting of a skirt called a "Kittel", blouse, jacket called a "Wannick", and an apron called a "Fietich".

Headscarf with Dotted Pattern (exhibit description)

In the background: a typical homemade head scarf. The dots were made using a template. This artistic craftsmanship died out in the Hutterite colonies.

Fur Hat for Winter and Boy's Cap (exhibit description)

(Far left in background)

These head-coverings hint at the unusual influence of non-Hutterite surroundings.

This fur cap as well as the boy's cap show Russian influence. Produced by "Lehrerleut" Hutterites.

Room B

The Three Branches of the Reformation

Teachings, Writing and Legacy
in Lower Austria

A World in Upheaval

The Middle Ages knew a variety of crises:

- Plague, locust swarms, and other natural catastrophes
- Diminishing honor in the Knighthood which lead to the Peasant Wars
- Threat of Turkish invasion
- Spiritual and religious insecurity through moral decay in spirituality
- The failure of attempts at Church reform (e.g. the Councils of Pisa, Constance, and Basel)
- Contradicting theological and practical directions (the scholastics, mystics, cults of relics, and lay piety.)

The Reformation

A renewal movement in Christianity had its beginning point in the 16th century.

As often in history, historical movements do not always begin at "zero hour;" we can look back at various precursors to the Reformation.

The Forerunners of the Reformation:

The Waldensians

12th to 15th centuries: they were named after the Lyon businessman named Peter Valdes. They were originally in the south of France and Italy. They were also particularly well represented in Austria (up to 50,000 people). Even to-day, there are scattered Waldensian communities in Italy.

John Wycliff

14th century, England: also known as the "morning star" of the Reformation. He translated parts of the Bible into his own language.

The Hussites

15th century, Bohemia: they trace their roots to reformer Jan Hus. He was burned at the stake on July 6, 1415. He blazed a trail for our freedom of con-science, which is often taken for granted today.

Section of the exhibition in Room B

The three "arch-heretics": Luther, Calvin, and Hubmaier

The Lutherans (Augsburg Confession)

Martin Luther (1483-1546)
Augustinian Monk and Theology Professor from Wittenberg

Luther was an Augustinian monk and theology professor from Wittenberg, Germany. He unleashed the Reformation with his 95 theses on October 31, 1517. Luther translated the Bible into German and used a popular and easily understandable language, making it a powerful cause of change. Among other influences, Luther's teachings caused medieval society to change permanently..

Martin Luther: Oil on canvas, artist unknown

Martin Luther formulated the four basic ideas of the Reformation:

- Sola scriptura: only the Holy Scripture is the basis of the Christian faith, not tradition.

- Solus Christus: Jesus Christ alone obtained salvation for sinful people through His saving work.

- Sola gratia: Only by the grace of God can a person be saved, not by his own deeds.

- Sola fide: Only through faith is a person justified, not by good works.

Luther's original motivation was the solution of a theological issue, namely, is God truly gracious?

Churches in the tradition of Martin Luther are the Protestant Lutheran Churches, for which the reformer Philipp Melanchthon drafted the Augsburg Confession on June 25, 1530 (Confessio Augustana).

The Reformed (Helvetic Confession)

Ulrich Zwingli (1484-1531)

Ulrich Zwingli (actually Huldrych Zwingli) is the reformer from Zurich. Among other places, he studied at the University of Vienna. At 22, he was ordained a priest and beginning in 1522, he published writings similar to other reformers. In 1523-1524, he defended his views before the city council of Zurich with his so-called "Zurich Disputations" against the accusation of heresy. Topics such as the worship of pictures, the catholic mass, and the celibacy of priests were on the agenda. Zwingli came out the winner of these debates, in which there were up to 900 religious and secular participants. Under his guidance, the Council provided schools, churches and families with a new code of moral conduct. While Luther only wanted to eliminate abuses in the church, he only accepted in the church what was explicitly in the Bible; therefore, he strictly banned pictures. Furthermore he also called for entirely new liturgies for church services. A new translation of the Bible (now called the "Zurich Bible") is accredited to him, in a heavily tinted Swiss-German. Zwingli was killed in 1531 in the Battle of Kappel.

Heinrich Bullinger (1504-1575) was Zwingli's successor in Zurich. He solidified the reformed faith and is regarded as the true founder of the **Protestant Reformed Church**. He was co-author of the **First Helvetic Confession** (1536).

Johannes Calvin (1509-1564)

John Calvin was a reformer of French origin. He developed his teachings mostly in Geneva. Calvin stressed the omnipotence of God with the doctrine of predestination and referred to the powerlessness of the human will. He required a strict morality and a high work ethic. Both were to be enforced by means of church discipline. The principles of the Christian church should, in his view, be expanded to the general community as well.

John Calvin, Oil on canvas, artist unknown

The teachings of Calvin united with those of Zwingli in the Protestant Re-
formed Church. Such Reformed Churches and communities are now outside
Switzerland, especially in the Netherlands, Scotland, Hungary, and Romania
(Transylvania). Also belonging to this branch of the Reformation is the Pres-
byterian Church and the Congregational Church. In Austria, the name of this
Confession is "Protestant Church, Helvetic Confession."

The Anabaptist Movement
(Forerunner of many free churches today)

**The Anabaptists formed the third branch of the Reformation, also called
the "Radical Reformation".**

They held the view that statements in the Bible regarding baptism describe only
the baptism of Christians mature in faith, based on their personal confession of
faith. The Anabaptists rejected the baptism of babies as unscriptural, which is
why they were put down by outsiders as "Re-baptizers" or "Anabaptists."

The origin of the movement was in Zurich, where their leaders wanted to consistently push ahead the process of reformation. There was a split from the
group surrounding Zwingli. The resulting Anabaptist movement was founded
January 21, 1525, when the first adult baptisms based on a personal confession of faith took place. Triggered by the expulsion from Zurich and numerous
persecutions, the Anabaptists spread rapidly through northern and southern
Germany, in today's Holland (East Friesland) and in Moravia. On February 24,
1527 the "Schleitheimer Articles" were finished by Michael Sattler (born
around 1495, executed on May 21, 1527), in which the teachings of the Anabaptists were systematically summarized.

In the Anabaptist movement, there was a variety of individuals who spread
their perspective through Central Europe. The following are some of them:

Konrad Grebel

He was born in 1498 and was a humanist academian who had studied in Vienna. He was the first adult to be baptized according to his faith. After his
release from captivity in 1526, he died from the plague.

Jörg Blaurock

a priest from Graubünden who was first to be Baptized according to his faith
by Grebel and worked as a missionary in Tirol. He was burned at the stake in
1529 in Klausen.

Jakob Hutter

from Tyrol was the leader of the Tyrolean Anabaptists. Later, he was extremely successful as a leader in Moravia. He was burned at the stake on February 25, 1536 in Innsbruck.

Balthasar Hubmaier

was born in 1485 and was originally a Roman Catholic priest. As a highly educated theologian, he was one of the leading personalities of the Anabaptist movement. In 1528, he was arrested in Vienna and burned alive. His motto was: "The truth cannot be killed."

Menno Simons

(1496-1561) was also a Roman Catholic priest. After a complete turnaround in his life, he became the founder of the peaceloving Mennonites who were named after him.

Anabaptists taught the strict separation of church and state, that is, they rejected the link between throne and altar and the idea of a national church.

Anabaptist teaching developed in its various forms – the sharing of all goods in common, strict isolation from the world, a policy of unconditional non-violence (love for one's enemies and patient suffering from injustice and violence) – a broad spectrum of Christian ethics. Their teaching emphasized the commandment from the Sermon on the Mount to love one's neighbor.

Due to the rigorous persecution of the whole Anabaptist movement from church and state, many of the leaders met their fate as martyrs. Only the Hutterites, Mennonites, and the Amish still exist today.

Other movements of later centuries carry on the key principles from the Anabaptists. Among them are the Baptists, the Brethren, and many other evangelical, free churches, now approximately one third of global Christianity.

Balthasar Hubmaier
"The truth cannot be killed!"

Balthasar Hubmaier, oil on canvas by Julia Kreuzspiegel, 2008

Theologian und Reformer

As he was burned at the stake in Vienna in 1528, he had already come a long way in his life of faith. As a Catholic priest, he was a worshipper of Mary and a pilgrimage preacher. He taught as a professor at the Universities of Freiburg and Ingolstadt.

Highly impressed by Luther's writings, in 1522 he contacted various reformed groups and began a friendship with Zwingli. In this environment he got to know the future Anabaptists Konrad Grebel and Felix Manz (later executed for their faith).

Hubmaier was baptized in 1525. Shortly thereafter, he was arrested in Zurich after having a fallout with Zwingli over his Anabaptist beliefs. Under threat of the death penalty he recanted his position and was able to flee to Nikolsburg, north of Vienna.

Zenith

In the following years in Nikolsburg, Hubmaier completed 18 written works, in which he was the first to develop a systematic theology of Anabaptist belief. Hubmaier played a particular role among the Anabaptists, because he stood against the use of force by both the ruling authorities and individual Christians. This led to arguments with Hans Hut, effecting the division of the Moravian Anabaptists into two groups, the "Stäbler" (Staff Carriers) and the "Schwertler" (Sword Carriers).

Captured at castle Kreuzenstein

In 1526 under the Habsburg Archduke Ferdinand, the Anabaptists in Moravia began to be persecuted. A year after his arrival in Nikolsburg, Hubmaier was arrested and led away to Vienna. Then they brought him and his wife to castle Kreuzenstein, just north of Vienna. The later bishop Fabri and the rector of the University of Vienna tried to persuade him to publicly renounce his faith.

Burned at the stake in Vienna

Despite use of torture, Hubmaier refused to renounce his teaching regarding baptism. He was subsequently sentenced to death on March 10, 1528 and was burned at the stake. His wife Elisabeth encouraged him until his death end to stay firm in his faith. Three days after his martyrdom she was thrown into the river from the Danube Bridge with a stone around her neck.

Counted with Luther and Calvin among the Arch Heretics

At the Council of Trent, Hubmaier was put on an equal footing with Luther and Calvin.

Hubmaier was the greatest theologian among the Anabaptists. He knew how to inspire his listeners as a talented, popular preacher who could bring the gospel to ordinary people.

The Development of the Confessions

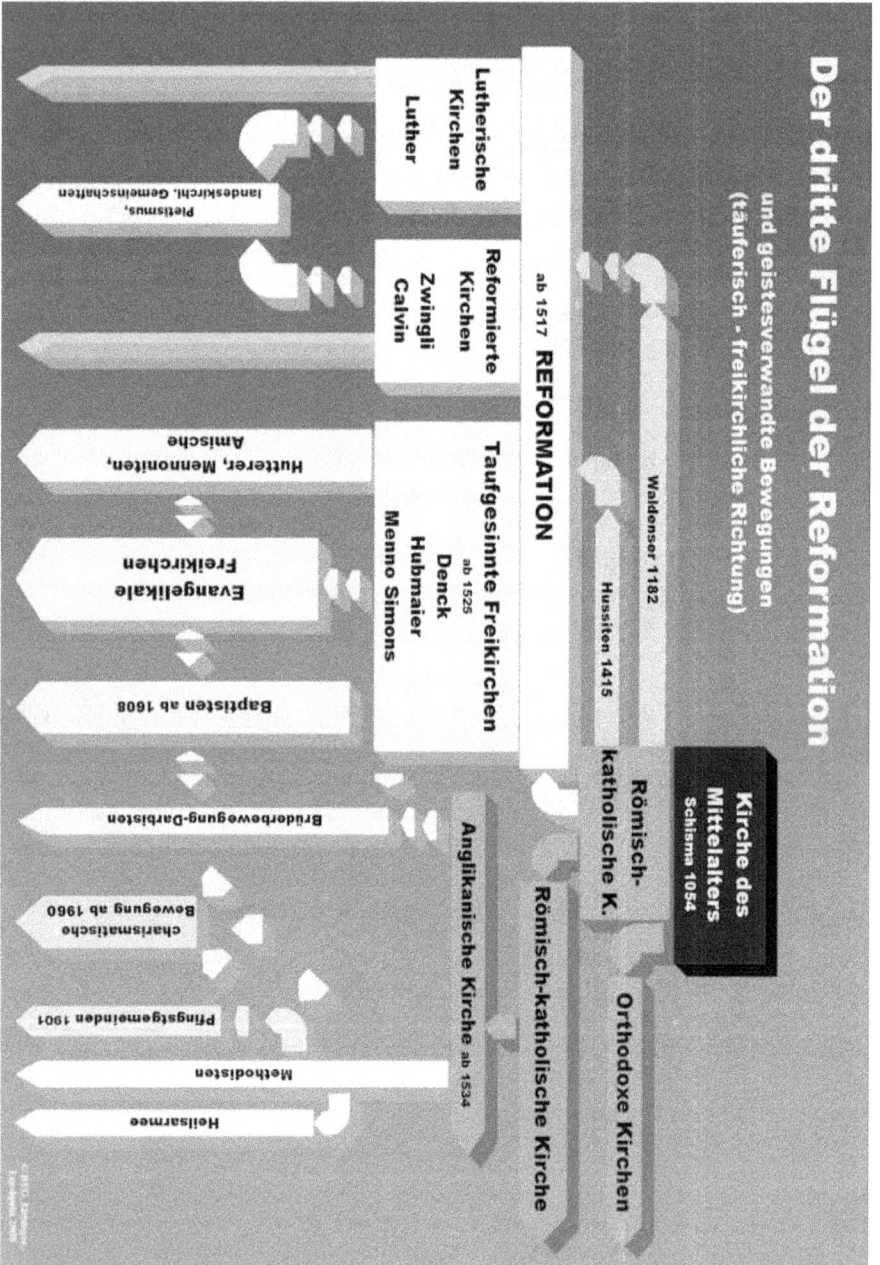

Der dritte Flügel der Reformation
und geistesverwandte Bewegungen
(täuferisch - freikirchliche Richtung)

Kirche des Mittelalters
Schisma 1054

Lutherische Kirchen
Luther

landeskirchl. Gemeinschaften,
Pietismus,

Reformierte Kirchen
Zwingli
Calvin

ab 1517 REFORMATION

Amische
Hutterer, Mennoniten,

Taufgesinnte Freikirchen
ab 1525
Denck
Hubmaier
Menno Simons

Evangelikale Freikirchen

Waldenser 1182

Hussiten 1415

Baptisten ab 1608

Brüderbewegung-Darbisten

charismatische Bewegung ab 1960

Römisch-katholische K.

Anglikanische Kirche ab 1534

Römisch-katholische Kirche

Orthodoxe Kirchen

Pfingstgemeinden 1901

Methodisten

Heilsarmee

Room B: View of three showcases

Konrad Grebel (1498-1526)

A "Lazy Student" becomes the father of a worldwide movement.

Konrad Grebel was the first "Anabaptist" mentioned in historical writings.

His father had good relations with the Habsburg family and the French king. His Swiss family never worried about money. This made studying in Vienna (1515-1518) and in Paris possible. He squandered his money for "stomach, books, and clothes" within three months. Though highly gifted, he got easily wrapped up in student life and even in fights, which finally kept him from earning a university degree. His parents called him back to Zurich in 1520.

But then came a radical life change. His study of the Bible changed his thinking and behavior. He was even able to argue Zwingli into a corner during various debates.

The issue of infant baptism is what separated him from Zwingli. Grebel believed that baptism is a conscious, free-will decision. On January 21, 1525, Grebel performed his first "re-baptism." The priest Georg Blaurock had requested to be baptized, after which Grebel himself was baptized.

But consequences didn't wait long. He was thrown into the tower of the city! With the help of his friends, however, he succeeded in escaping.

The plague brought the 28-year-old to an abrupt end.

In his own opinion, he would have preferred to testify of his convictions of faith with his own blood. However, sometimes it only takes a few years to become the "Father of a Movement."

(*D.G. Lichdi*, Konrad Grebel und die frühe Täuferbewegung; *H.-J. Goertz*, Konrad Grebel. Kritiker des frommen Scheins)

Baptism Was the Crux of the Matter!

On January 21, 1525 a serious decision with difficult consequences was made in Zurich.

The first voluntary baptism since the early church took place according to one's personal faith.

Konrad Grebel and Felix Mantz were students of Zwingli. Grebel had studied a few years in Vienna (as had Zwingli). Through Bible study he came to recognize that baptism was always the result of faith and not vice versa.

The practice of infant baptism was thus a problem. As early as 1524 in Zurich, some had refused to allow their babies to be baptized. The city council subsequently ordered the baptism of all newborns. Even Zwingli in his public "Disputations" could no longer convince his students to accept infant baptism. Tensions were high in the city!

The Hutterite Chronicle describes further events:

> "... because they have begun to bend their knees before the highest God ...because they knew what they must tolerate and suffer.
>
> ... After prayer Georg got up and left Jacob's house and in obedience to the will of God, asked Conrad Grebel to baptize him with the proper Christian baptism according to his faith and understanding. Because he knelt with such desire and longing, Grebel baptized him, since no other minister was there to do this work. At this point others desired to be baptized just like Georg."

With this step, the former students of Zwingli became persecuted heretics just like the other fathers of the Anabaptist movement.

Not Everyone Was Baptized!

The Anabaptists baptized only after a clear conversion and a public confession of faith. Baptism was for them the confirming, outward sign of turning one's heart to Christ.
Peter Riedemann wrote in 1565 about the prerequisites of baptism:

> *"The one to be baptized must first desire, ask for, and earnestly seek [baptism] before he can be baptized."*

Leonhard Schiemer said in 1527::

> *"By way of summary: Water-baptism is a confirmation of faith and an unswerving covenant with God. Just like when one writes a letter...and afterwards want to have that letter officially sealed [with wax]; but no one will certify or seal it, before he knows what's in the letter. He who baptizes a child certifies an empty letter."*
>
> (Lydia Müller (Hg.), Quellen zur Geschichte der Täufer Bd.III)

Neither the baptizers nor those baptized shared their names!

This was a security measure. Even under the most extreme torture it was impossible to betray others.

The outward procedure of baptism was not so important to the Anabaptists. They looked for all kinds of opportunities. People were baptized in rivers, barns, and parlors. It wasn't possible to baptize everywhere with full immersion.

Those baptized were often quickly put on death row for being baptized.

*   Eucharius Binder went through Nürnberg to Steyr in 1525. On his way he baptized a few hundred people. One year later, at 37 years of age, he was burned at the stake with other Anabaptists.

*   Leonhard Dorfbrunner, a young knight, baptized over 3,000 others in the city of Steyr inside of one year after his own baptism. (He was beaten and burned at the stake in 1528 in Passau.)

*   Leenaerdt Boewens in Holland baptized 9,000, according to his own writings. In comparison: Vienna had 25,000 inhabitants in 1530.

Forerunners of the Separation of Church and State

Today it's almost taken for granted in democracies, that church and state should be separate. It wasn't always this way. Both church and state reacted to people who had a dissenting view of faith with a fierceness which can hardly be exaggerated. No one dared to question the intertwining of church and state – until the Anabaptists came along.

They were one of those first movements in early modernity who denied the connection of church and state. These Anabaptists wanted to live out their personal faith independent from the state's decrees.

At the beginning of this development was theologian Dr. Balthasar Hubmaier, who was executed in Vienna in 1528. In his tracts he condemned all use of force in questions of religion. His writing "Of Heretics and their Executioners" is one of the first calls for tolerance to be written in Europe.

Tiara of the Pope and the German Kaiser's crown

At the same time, the family of Habsburgs defended the Roman Catholic, papal church. The Anabaptists were declared to be political enemies, since through their ideas they endangered the common Roman Catholic power over society.

Tolerance and Freedom of Conscience were unknown in the 16th century. Freedom often ended up on a pyre. Even among the Turks there was more religious freedom than under the Habsburgs!

However, the Lutherans and Calvinists held firmly to the character of the church (in national churches). Soon they proved themselves in their own regions to be as intolerant as the Catholics. Luther and Zwingli even wrote reports on heretics!

Among the first immigrants in North America there were many religious refugees from Europe including Anabaptists! The idea of the separation of Church and State was holy to them. The first amendment to the United States constitution reads: "Congress shall make no law respecting an establishment of religion…"

A lack of tolerance for religious minorities can also be found today! The Society for Inter-religious Understanding and Cooperation constantly raises awareness regarding problem.

Hubmaier-memorial plaque, 1st district of Vienna by Stubentor

Getting Away from National Churches – Back to the Church of Confessing Believers

Caspar Braitmichel, one of the co-authors of the Hutterite Chronicles, got to the crux of the issue of the voluntary nature of faith in 1530:

> *"Belief should not to forced, for it is a gift of God. As Christ speaking to his disciple said: 'Will anyone follow me (see, someone wants to and desires it!), he must deny himself and take up his cross.'"*

Faith is not automatic for everyone. Therefore, the church cannot be a church of the broad masses! Only a community of those who want to follow Christ voluntarily can be the true church of God! For the Anabaptists this was clear.

This later became the understanding of most free churches.

All reformers strongly highlighted the meaning of personal faith with brings salvation. Ultimately, however, it was only the Anabaptists who managed to require that each local church be composed only of people whose faith was voluntary. They thought it was pointless that high numbers of nominal followers had dominated the state church since the time of Emperor Constantine. They wanted to call the masses in national churches to faith and to gather them in churches of voluntary believers.

At the same time, this was a radical break with the ruling leaders of society.

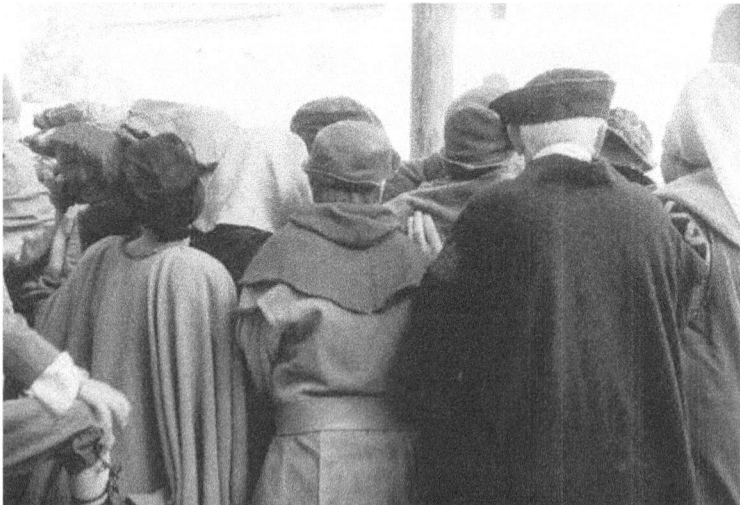

From the film "Jakob Hutter and the Hutterites"

Just Emulate Jesus –
A Theology for Practical Living

> *"None may truly know Christ unless he follows Him with his life."*
> Hans Denk, 16th century, Anabaptist from Augsburg

The Bible was just as important to the Anabaptists as it was to other reformers. They made the lives of individuals their central concern. Faith must have an effect on one's daily life. The law of love had to go from the head and heart to the fingertips and feet in order to serve one's fellow man.

The practical, ethical lifestyle of the Anabaptists was often their strongest apologetic, albeit unintentionally so.

In 1582, the Catholic theologian Franz Agricola wrote the following:

> *Among the heretical sects there is none that live such a humble and godly life toward outsiders as the Anabaptists. They are blameless in their external life. They don't lie, they don't swear oaths, they don't fight, and they don't speak with evil words. They avoid gluttony and drinking. One finds in them modesty, patience, sincerity, cleanliness, moderation, and honesty in such extent that you almost have to accept that they have the Holy Spirit of God.*

(From the first protestant lawsuit against various atrocious errors
of the Anabaptists)

From the film "Jakob Hutter and the Hutterites"

Die Täufer und die Bibel

In die Gefängnisse konnte man fast nie Bibeln mitnehmen.
Zu Ketzerverhören wurden Theologen oft von weit herbeigeholt. Dennoch konnten diese, was die Schriftkenntnis betraf, gegen die einfachen Täufer häufig argumentativ nicht viel ausrichten.

Der Begriff „sola scriptura" war von Luther und Zwingli geprägt worden.
Den Täufern ging es aber darüber hinaus um mehr als ein theologisches Prinzip. Ihr Ziel war die Verinnerlichung der Heiligen Schrift und die gelebte Gemeinschaft mit Christus.

Balthasar Hubmaier schrieb 1528, bevor er in Wien verbrannt wurde:

„Ohne Zweifel hören viele Leute das Wort Gottes äußerlich, verstehen es aber innerlich nicht. Da ist es Not zu beten und Weisheit zu begehren von Gott im Glauben."

(G. Mecenseffy, Quellen zur Geschichte der Täufer)

Section of the exhibition in Room B.

The Anabaptists and the Bible

They couldn't take any Bibles with them into prison. During hearings theologians were often brought from a long way away. The imprisoned Anabaptists were often at a disadvantage, since they had to argue their case without a Bible.

The term "sola scriptura" was developed by Luther and Zwingli. But for the Anabaptists, the concept involved much more than simply a theological principle; its goal was to make the Scriptures a part of oneself and to be a means of fellowship with Christ.

Balthasar Hubmaier wrote the following before he was burned at the stake in Vienna, 1528:
"No doubt many people hear the word of God outwardly, but inwardly don't understand it. Therefore it is urgent to pray and to earnestly seek wisdom from God in faith."

(G. Mecenseffy, Quellen zur Geschichte der Täufer)

"All Old Testament Prophets:
Translation into German from the Original Hebrew"

The pocketbook edition of the Old Testament prophets by Anabaptists Hans Denck and Ludwig Hätzer was printed at Worms by Peter Schöffer on September 7, 1527.

It was the first translation from Hebrew to German. Luther criticized it initially, since they had taken Jewish recommendations into consideration. He later used it, however, as a reference for his own translation.

The handy format of this edition gave Anabaptist missionaries an advantage, since this part of the Bible could easily be hidden. The prophetic books of the Bible were also highly valued in this period of increased awareness of the immanency of Christ's return.

The binding of the original came from the Hutterites, more specifically from Isaac Dreller, who replaced the cover of the well-read book around 1650.

This shows that this small book was in use by the Hutterites even 130 years after its printing.

Room B: replica of a small book

The First Doctrine-Oriented Foundation:
The Schleitheimer Confession

Anabaptists completed their first written confession of faith three years before the Lutherans finished their "Augsburg Confession."

In the small Swiss locale of Schleitheim, the "Brotherly Union" (also known as the "Schleitheimer Articles") was founded.

They kept themselves inside the framework of the Apostolic Creed.

The following points were defined.

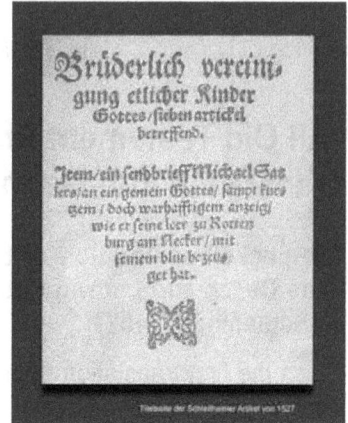

Section of an exhibition display, title page from "Brotherly Union of Many Children of God / regarding 7 articles" Schleitheim, 1527

1. Baptism should only be applied to those who are ready to follow Jesus Christ voluntarily.

2. The only means to punish wrongdoing in the church is through exclusion or through church discipline.

3. The Lord's Supper will be understood as a supper of remembrance. Bread stays bread, wine stays wine – they are symbols that remind us of Christ's flesh and blood.

4. The doctrine of separation: The Anabaptists recognized the difference between the kingdom of God and the "World." Their lifestyle should be clearly different than that of unbelievers.

5. The church should be led by shepherds who live out an exemplary lifestyle of leadership and should be chosen by the local church.

6. The section "Of the sword" described why a Christian should not hold a government position and should never serve in the military.

7. The last article concerned the refusal of oaths. This included the ordinary oaths of faithfulness to local princes and others.

Much of what earlier church reform movements had stipulated was put in place by the Anabaptists.

The Celebration of the Lord's Supper by the Anabaptists

The Anabaptists practiced voluntary fellowship which knew no clergy. This was reflected in the celebration of the Lord's Supper.

- **The practice of the Lord's Supper was uncomplicated.**
  A few words of introduction were spoken out of the New Testament. Then the people took everyday bread and distributed it among themselves along with wine.
  "The striking thing in this scene is its apostolic simplicity."

  "The meaning of the Lord's Supper was three-fold:
  – the duty to a Christian lifestyle
  – the duty of love toward God
  – the symbolism of the bond between Christians."
  Fritz Blanke, Brüder in Christo

- **The Lord's Supper was seen as a supper of remembrance.**
  Bread and wine reminded them symbolically of the body and blood of Christ. They remembered Christ's sacrifice on the cross, his payment for the sin of mankind.

- **The Hutterites considered the Lord's Supper to be the biggest event of the year.**
  Thousands came, most often at Easter, for two days. Many talked with Elders about their sins, confessing them, since no one was to take part in the Lord's Supper with unconfessed sin.

On Military Service at the Brink of War

The German Peasants' War of 1524-1525 had only just ended. The Turkish army crept ever closer (1st Turkish siege of Vienna, 1529).

During this time, the message of the Anabaptist Michael Sattler seemed particularly alien when he said, "Give the Turks no resistance." For Sattler, the only thing that counted was the Sermon on the Mount of Jesus Christ and His commandment to love one's enemies. In 1527, Sattler was tried as a heretic; this statement was used as a point of indictment.

The question of whether self-defense was allowed for a Christian and whether it was right to take up arms in defense of the state divided the young movement in Nikolsburg (Mikulov) into two camps, the **"Schwertler"** (Sword Carriers) and the **"Stäbler"** (Staff Carriers).

The latter group took the radical stance of "defenselessness" (pacifism) and eventually had to leave Nikolsburg. From this group, a smaller group of Tyrolean refugees in Auspitz (Hustopece) formed **the first Hutterite church**.

They were called "Staff Carriers" because their only resort to persecution was to flee from their persecutors, walking staff in hand. Their walking staffs had to be taken up many times. The Hutterite Brethren have made many stops in their history of fleeing persecution.

In Russia they were allowed to live in peace for a long time. However, in the 19th century during the rise of Russian nationalism, conditions changed and the defenseless Hutterites would have been forced to serve in the military.

In 1874 they took their walking staffs in hand and moved to South Dakota (USA).

In the course of World War I, their strict position of pacifism renewed their conflict with political reality. Many young Hutterites who refused to serve in the military were put in US military prisons. Two of them died from abuse they suffered there.

Because of this persecution, they once again reached for their walking staffs and moved north into Canada.

Through their consistent position against military service, for reasons of conscience, Hutterite and Mennonite forerunners paved the way for a consistent pacifism.

Today we have the possibility [in Austria] of civil service instead of military service.

One Who Loved His Enemy

A picture is worth a thousand words!! Copper engraving by Jan Luiken
in the so-called "Märthyrer Spiegel" (Martyr's Mirror)

This image and the accompanying story have travelled around the world, not through the mass media, but by the telling of the narrative by those who have been inspired by it. Today you can find this picture on the internet by searching for "Dirk Willems;" where you can read the whole story.

In 1569 the Dutch Anabaptist Dirk Willems fled from his persecutor over a frozen river. His persecutor fell into the ice behind him. Was this the just punishment of God? The Anabaptists had learned not to think that way. Jesus said that we should do good to those who hate us. What good could Willems do for his pursuer? He saved his life. However, he lost his own life, because in spite of his readiness to make peace and to love his enemy he was burned at the stake.

"The truth cannot be killed!"

was the motto of the theologian Dr. Balthasar Hubmaier, the greatest Anabaptist theologian. With this statement he expressed his new-found confidence of the indestructibility of the truth of the gospel.

This said Hubmaier:

"The truth cannot be killed and though they've been looking for it a long time in order to scourge, crown, crucify, and bury it in the grave...even so on the third day it will rise again victorious, reigning, and triumphant."

(Dr. Balthasar Hubmaier, "A sincere, Christian offering," 1524.)

BALTHASAR HUBMOR DOCTOR VON FRIDBERG

Dr. Balthasar Hubmaier. One should note the two scenes of execution in the background

Nikolsburg Becomes
the Stronghold of the Anabaptists

The castle of Nikolsburg (Mikulov) is still enthroned with pride over the same-named city, close to the border of Lower Austria.

With the arrival of Dr. Balthasar Hubmaier in July 1526, it became the strong-hold of the Anabaptists.

Simprecht Sorg, a book printer, who took Hubmaier with him from Zurich, began to set up a printing shop immediately. Its goal was to serve as the main source for the distribution of countless Anabaptist writings.

Hubmaier, a powerful speaker, could build on the favor of the lords of Liech-tenstein. Even Prince Leonhard of Liechtenstein was baptized in his own resi-dent city "among a lot of people."

By Hubmaiers's down-to-earth preaching, Nikolsburg and its surroundings quickly became extraordinarily popular. A total of 12,000 religious refugees settled there. The devout from today's Austria and half of Europe were under the protection of the Prince.

A whole section of the city around the Predigtstuhl Street and the upper Steinzeile Street were obviously carved out of the ground by many feet (see map). The houses are similar to the one which holds Anabaptist Museum in Niedersulz.

Nikolsburg was the starting point for a good 50 more localities of the later Hutterite branch of the Anabaptist movement.

Even in Vienna the clergy complained about many pilgrims going to Nikolsburg. The whole situation became a thorn in the flesh of the government of Vienna. By royal command, the Protestant prince had to deliver his treasured theolo-gian, Balthasar Hubmaier, who was burned at the stake in Vienna in 1528.

Later in Vienna, other important Anabaptist leaders from Nikolsburg were executed, such as Jakob Wiedemann and Oswald Glaidt.

Prince Cardinal Franz von Dietrichstein, the new lord of Nikolsburg, took it upon himself in 1622 to "eradicate all heretics out of his territory." In that year, all Anabaptists were forced to either become Catholic or to leave the area empty-handed. Even a dwelling for the sick through the winter was not al-lowed. Soon the pompous Corpus Christi processions went through the former streets of the Anabaptists.

The "The Augsburg Synod of Martyrs" – Survival Rate for Participants Two Years at Most

In 1527, there was a meeting at Augsburg, which has been known in history as the "Synod of Martyrs," since almost all of the 60 participants were martyred within two years thereafter.

The purpose of the synod was to bring a consensus to the young and rapidly growing Anabaptist movement. A strong emphasis on apocalyptic ideas was rejected, in spite of the plague and the threat of Turkish invasion.

Nevertheless, the group was unanimous in its belief that Christ would soon return. This is why pairs of missionaries were sent out to each area of Europe, each to a precisely allotted section.

Three months after the synod the first pyres burned in the market places at Augsburg, Salzburg, Weissenberg, Vienna, Passau, and Linz. In the same year, Leonhard Schiemer was killed in Rattenberg am Inn. Hans Schlaffer was beheaded in Schwaz, Tyrol. One of the synod participants was a particularly influential preacher named Hans Hut.

Community Property over Centuries

Sharing to Set an Example

There were tensions between rich and poor even in the 15th and 16th centuries.The response of the Anabaptists to social differences, like social status and ownership, is directly related to their perception of the biblical church of Christ:

> "... the holy community should be recognized not only in spiritual things but also in temporal things, so that, just as Paul said, no one should have plenty when another has deficiency."
>
> Peter Riedemann, "Accountability," from around 1550

Hutterites, especially those who had just fled from Tyrol and other areas, chose the path of communal property. In this way the Hutterites created an alternative culture.

Their families have attempted to live this way for over 500 years, though with increasing financial success there were often difficulties and tensions between them.

Today it is said of the Hutterites that they have the world's only viable long term model of a functioning "communism."

The Hutterite Edward Kleinsasser adds:

> *"There is only one answer to this: God must be present; otherwise it wouldn't work."*

Anabaptists in Lower Austria

In almost every larger town in Lower Austria the Anabaptists left traces of their presence. Much of their 16th century beginnings we learn from their meeting notes and the Hutterite Chronicles.

Northeast of Lower Austria was the region of Moravia, which was the key center of the movement, with at least 20,000 people!

Hans Hut, Oswald Glaidt, and Leonhard Schiemer were the first Anabaptist leaders in Lower Austria. The movement appears to have begun quickly in 1526. For example, when Hut came to Waldegg, the local clergy who housed him already had 100 Anabaptists associated with them.

King Ferdinand was disgruntled because his harsh mandate wasn't strictly enforced. Thus, he put his own men in place and in 1528 alone there were at least 91 executions in Lower Austria.

The constant persecution of the Anabaptist movement did not give it any chance to establish itself. Communities were often robbed of their leaders and then dispersed. Often new members kept moving further towards Moravia. Even while travelling, Anabaptists were driven out of their temporary quarters, being pushed further on to Retz and even back to the Danube River.

The "Land beyond the Enns [River]" became a place to simply pass through. In their region there were "stowaways" who for missionary reasons or out of financial desperation stayed in this area. In order to more easily catch a "heretic," in 1534 the authorities mandated a "general enforcement of confession." Those who refused had to be immediately turned in to the authorities.

In 1625 under Ferdinand II, policy still required everyone to
> *become and remain Catholic or leave.*

Gradually, most people succumbed to external pressure. These men and women were called Habans. Ultimately, many were established as craftsmen in this region and simply became of part of Lower Austrian society.

Examples like these are countless

- In **Hadres** (Niederhollabrunn) Wilhelm von Kuenring had four Anabaptists captured. Four recanted. An "old woman," however, remained stubborn and was burned to death at royal command.

- In 1536 **Mödling**, the Anabaptists missionaries Georg Fasser and Lienhard Lanzenstiel were captured, but were freed by free by a stroke of "luck." But four more executions followed.

- In **Melk**, Joerg Krautschlögel, a tax collector who had been driven out of Vienna, baptized 400 people.

- In **Pöggstall,** a community of Anabaptists wanted to come together. Georg Fasser was sent to them. He preached with success, was, however, later captured. After surviving torture, he was executed. Others in his area escaped to Moravia.

- In **Stein near Krems,** whole travelling parties were caught on their way to Moravia. Usually only the leader was put on trial.

- In **Laa an der Thaya**, citizens were punished because they hired Anabaptists to mow grass in their fields.

- In **Krems** the Anabaptists were so strong and numerous including the nobility, that the city council was publicly shamed.

- From **Retz** came Andreen Keller Maier who was rooted out in Tyrol by a spy and was arrested.

- In **Ottenschlag** in 1712, there are reports of two "Anabaptists" whose children were baptized Catholic.

- In **Eggenburg**, a group led by Bastl Glaser was arrested, their backs burned, and then were let go.

- In **Traiskirchen** an Anabaptist was driven out in 1552.

The Anabaptists of Lower Austria.

The Golden Apple

One of Many Legends about the Hutterites

The Hutterites were always a bit secretive in what they did. This encouraged the formation of many legends about them. Most of them deal with their underground caves and their treasures. The following is an example:

"When the Anabaptists left Landshut (at Bernhardsthal), they had to leave all their belongings behind. What they could hide, they buried in their cellars. It is reported, that when leaving, they asked whether they could at least take apples with them. Their request was granted; they were allowed to take apples in already fully loaded wagons.

On their way to Slovakia, the March River stood in their way. For the crossing they had no money, but they hoped for the goodness of the ferry captain, that he might bring them over the river for free. They waited a few days until the captain finally brought them to the other shore. As payment they offered him delicious apples, from which he should take as many as he wanted.

The ferry captain didn't want any at first, but he finally took two of them. The Anabaptists were taken by boat to the nearest Slovak community, to Brodske. The ferry captain got thirsty, and so after taking a hearty bite, he almost broke his old teeth. In the apple had been hidden a golden ducat. And when he broke open the other apple, he found another golden ducat. He then ran after the Habans, shouting that he really would like a few more apples. But they paid no attention to him."

There is always a little bit of truth to be found in these legends, since the Hutterites were really quite wealthy. Czech soil may still hold tremendous treasures from these rebels of faith,

"...including the depths of the Mountain Vetrover, under the Church of Pavlovice, in a cellar of Damborice or below the house number 13 in Rakvice, where the Anabaptists hid two vats of coins," and so on...

The search can begin!

To symbolize the apple legend, an artificial apple is displayed behind glass.

However, when the Hutterites spoke of "their true treasure" (singular), they meant something else. This treasure was, in their eyes, a lot more valuable than gold! In the next room you will find in an old quote as a hint.

"The search can begin!", from Adolf Mais, "The Anabaptist Saga"

From the Thaya and March Rivers to the Shore of the Missouri

- After the Battle of White Mountain, the Hutterites fled from Moravia to Upper Hungary.

- They lived in Transylvania until a great persecution occurred in the 1750's. Many Jesuit priests came during that time, too, and attempted to turn them back to Catholicism.

- The Transylvanian Hutterites, who were strengthened in number in 1775 from fleeing Carinthians, moved to Wallachia in 1767 and finally into northern Ukraine. A lifestyle of shared property was used again, though causing many disagreements.

- In 1842 these Hutterites moved to southern Ukraine's Molotschna where they were helped by Mennonites to create their own settlements. In the 1870's Russian nationalism increased dramatically; as a result the pacifistic Hutterites were forced to serve in the military.

- In 1874, the Hutterites and other Mennonite groups chose to leave instead of serve military duty, moving to South Dakota in the United States.

- During World War I, they came again in conflict with politics, since military duty was required of all American men. Many young Hutterites were imprisoned for refusing military duty. Two even died in prison from severe abuse. These Hutterites subsequently moved to the north from there into **Canada**.

Migration for the Sake of Faith

The Lutherans and Hutterites Shared the Same Fate

Archbishop Leopold Anton Freiherr von Firmian decreed emigration in 1731. Twenty-two thousand Protestants were driven out of Salzburg. Despite of the coming winter, they were forced to leave. Some went to Prussia, while others settled in North America. Many did not survive the difficult travel.

In spite of the fate of expulsion, Lutherans and Anabaptists formed a spiritual union in 1755. Those driven out of Carinthia went to Transylvania where underground Protestants took in the refugees, which apparently accounts for their survival.

Original signet for wax of Archbishop Firmian.

High Season for Flyers and Writings

The spiritual dawn in Europe came through the invention of the printing press. The Anabaptists used this modern technology to spread their message. For example, Balthasar Hubmaier took with him to Nikolsburg a talented printer named Simprecht Sorg.

Many Anabaptist writings were written in prisons – without libraries or reference books. The writings spread like wildfire. Catholics publicly burned these Anabaptist works, and Luther, Zwingli, and Bucer wrote sharp rebuttals to these [Anabaptist publications].

The nobility feared their influence more than the power of an enemy army. The publication, distribution, and even the possession of Anabaptist writings was a capital crime.

Hans Denk and Ludwig Hätzer translated the Prophets of the Old Testament. This was the first translation from Hebrew into German. Luther criticized them directly, since they took Jewish teachers' suggestions into consideration. Later, he himself used them as a guideline for his own translation.

Flyers Forbidden in Vienna

"On June 24, 1528, Ferdinand I decreed that all printers and sellers of Brethren sects be drowned and their books burned."

Theodor Wiedmann, Geschichte der Reformation und Gegenreformation im Lande unter der Enns, Volume 1, Prague 1879, page 61

On March 10, 1528, Dr. Balthasar Hubmaier was burned at the stake because of his baptistic way of thinking.

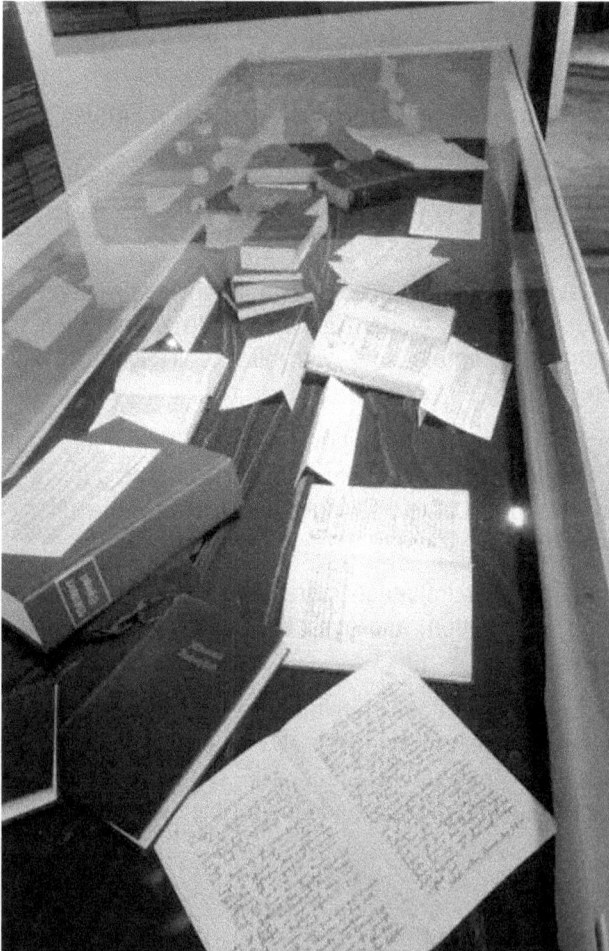

Showcase with pamphlets and Anabaptist literature.

Of Heretics, Who Have "their own king, a leader like other outlaws"

The Hutterite Dovecote

"The Hutterite-Anabaptist's Dovecote: In which is all their rotting hair, rubbish, dung, and filth, the same of which is their stinking, filthy, and abhorrent doctrine."

So read the title of a polemic leaflet by Christoph Andreas Fischer, who began to write against the Hutterites in 1607.

Christoph Andreas Fischer, a priest in the then Lower Austrian town of Feldsberg (today's Valtice), was a critic of the close relationship of the Moravian land owners with their Hutterite subjects. According to Fischer, they would rather do business with Hutterite businesses than with Catholic ones.

This strong and controversy-inspiring writing betrayed some insider knowledge, such as:

"Among the sects that have come out of Luther's teaching, there isn't one better looking with a greater outer holiness than the Anabaptists. Other sects are mostly rebellious, makeshift, and given to fleshly lusts, but not the so-called Anabaptists. They call each other Brother and Sister, they don't curse, steal, swear oaths, and don't need any armor or weapons. They don't gorge themselves nor do they need clothes that are pompous like the world. They don't privately own anything, but share everything. They don't kiss up to authorities and are patient in everything, as they say, in the Holy Spirit.

...Who would believe that there would be wolves in sheep's clothing among them?"

Fischer fomented the professional jealousy of craftsmen who could not compete with Hutterite products.

At the same time his report of the legendary riches of the Hutterites, which they supposedly hoarded, caused the following fabrication:

"The heretics – contrary to the authorities – have their own king, a leader like other outlaws, who alone knows where all these riches are hidden."

Constant pillaging was the result.

The "Hutterite Dovecote" shows a Hutterite couple standing in front of a dovecote (a structure for housing domesticated pigeons.) The poles of the dovecote are covered with symbols of various trades in which the Hutterites worked. Tailors, bakers, rope makers, and sock knitters. The man is holding a jug in his hand which hints at the Hutterites ceramic production. Bats fly around the dovecote.

Allegedly, Fischer wanted to connect the Hutterites with Alchemy and Astrology. This propaganda leaflet compared the houses of the Anabaptists with dovecotes: *these people are full of bad advice and live on the best property in the country, though their places are full of holes and nests* – probably a play on the small sleeping berths in the roofs of their farm houses. A dovecote with multiple levels was the early hub of the Hutterite farmstead.

From the title page of an inflammatory pamphlet by Christoph A. Fischer, 1607. Here are shown the various coats of arms of the guilds whose trades the Anabaptists practiced.

Rediscovered: The History Book from the Losers!

It is well known, that "history is written by the victors." But the Hutterites wrote their own history themselves with great care.

The so-called "Thick Book," hand-written by Hutterites, tells their story in journal style up until 1665. It starts with the creation of the earth, the history of the chosen people, the apostles, and the model of the devout over the centuries.

To encourage themselves in steadfastness of faith, the faith testimonies of martyrs are the central theme of the "Thick Book."

This book has its own history, too!

The Hutterite Kaspar Braitmichel began to write in Moravia and continued the "Bichl" until 1542. Since then, a list of various writers has contributed to the work.

This history book accompanied the Brethren from Moravia into Slovakia, and later escaped the watchful eyes of the Jesuits in the Transylvanian Brethren community in Winz. From there it was smuggled into the prison at Hermannstadt. Martin Glanzer then brought it to Wischenky from where it was taken to southern Russia by an unknown person, and finally by someone in 1874 to the prairies of the United States, when the Hutterites immigrated there. Austrian historians believed by the middle of the 19th century that the Hutterites had been wiped out and their history book lost!

The original book is 1,000 pages long. Today it lies in the Bon-Homme colony of the "Schmiedeleut" in South Dakota. A revised edition of the "History Book," edited by Rudolf Wolkan in 1923, is still easily accessible.

History Book: Bon Homme Colony;.

The original History Book of the Hutterite brethren, Bon-Homme Colony

The Martyrs' Mirror (Der Märtyrerspiegel)

Original German title translates as follows: "The bloodly setting or martyrs' mirror of baptistic and defenseless Christians who have suffered for their testimony of Jesus who is their source of all joy, and have been killed since the time of Christ until the year 1660."

The "Martyrs Mirror", originally a 10cm / 4inch thick, heavy leather-bound book, is one of the main sources of Anabaptist history.

It was edited by the Dutchman Thieleman Jansz van Braght in 1660.

Jan Luiken contributed to it for its second printing in 1685 with his famous etchings which lend this chronicle a special vibrancy.

From 1748-1750 the first German edition appeared in Pennsylvania, USA.

In one of these engravings, the "Falkenstein martyrs" are displayed.

In the glass-case: Sixth German edition in high German from 1870, Pennsylvania, USA.

The "Ausbund"

The "Ausbund" is the oldest songbook of the Anabaptists. It was created in the areas of southern Germany and Austria. The main section comprises 51 songs that were written between 1535 and 1537 from the castle prison of Passau. The poets remained faithful to their faith in spite of torture.

Originally it was copied by hand or distributed in print as flyers, which strengthened the faith of many generations of Anabaptists over the centuries.

Today, the Amish in Pennsylvania (USA) still sing songs out of the "Ausbund", the oldest songbook of the Anabaptists (see example).

Message from a Castle Dungeon

What was important to the authors?

H.B., probably Hans Betz, composed a song in 1530 from a castle dungeon, out of which he never came alive:

*I fell away from God through sin
and came into His wrath;
Nevertheless He has given me a new birth
and made me His child,
in His son the Lord Jesus Christ,
who also has become my mediator,
so that I will not be lost.*

Ausbund (Songbook) Song no. 112, stanza 17

Books of Sermons

Andreas Ehrenpreis began in 1639 to develop standard sermons for all occasions.
These sermons were gathered in handwritten
books and soon thereafter, most sermons
were simply read out loud.

This practice still exists among the Hutterites. Almost every preacher has copies of
such sermons, most of them from that period.

The thought behind this practice: The nature
of mankind has not changed and everything
has already been said.

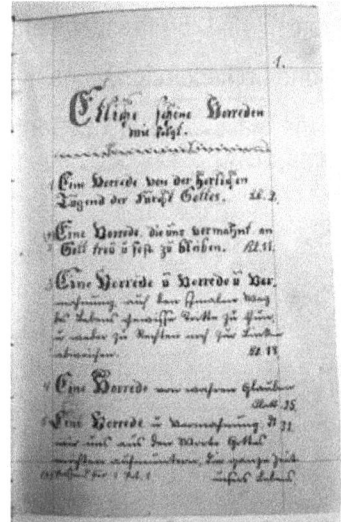

Original example of one of
many hand-written sermon
books

Room C

Daily Life and Cultural Activities, Language, and Artisanry of the Anabaptists

View of room C

Life in a Community Settlement (Bruderhof)

In 1528, in Austerlitz, Moravia, the first Hutterite settlement was established, which practiced "community of goods" (the ownership of all material possessions in common). They lived, worked, and ate together.

In these communities an average of 500 people lived together. These communities, of which there were soon over 70 in number, consisted of various houses, a school, dining-hall, infirmary, and various trade shops. These communities were usually on the edge of larger settlements and towns. Each community was almost entirely self-sufficient.

Divison of Labour

- Each community had at least one "Steward of the Word" who acted as chaplain and pastor in spiritual matters.

- The "Steward of the House" was responsible for business matters. He administrated the community's finances and was responsible for business matters outside the settlement.

- Special buyer/sellers procured all necessary raw materials and oversaw the sale of goods produced in the settlement.

- The education of children was also accomplished communally. Each child could learn the trade which fit him the best and for which he was physically capable.

For each type of industry, governing rules were put in place.

Even married couples had only small berths for sleeping.

Private space was tight. For singles there were large sleeping quarters for multiple people. Nursing babies were often separated from their parents after just six weeks and put in a nursery, where their mothers visited them three times daily to nurse them.

The whole life of the community was thoroughly religious. Widows and orphans were cared for and the unemployed and sick were supported.

In many Brethren communities there were spinning rooms
which produced textiles of excellent quality.

The "Golden Age" in Moravia

Southern Moravia was the "the promised land" for the Anabaptist movement.
The protestant lords hoped to use Anabaptist settlers as a means of increasing their wealth.

The new inhabitants were tradesmen of much better quality than their neighbors because of both their skill and hard work. They only earned, however,
about 1/3 the average wage of other people, but did have religious freedom
and protection.

These conditions attracted many other Anabaptists. The flow of religious refugees from Tyrol and other areas in the empire toward Moravia didn't let up.
Twenty-five thousand Hutterites lived in Neumühl, which was 10% of the
whole population of Moravia! The area of Znaim-Lundenburg-Wischau developed into a Hutterite center with nearly 70 communities at its peak.

The years of 1565-1592 are known as the "Golden Age." During this time
there was no persecution, and in spite of high taxation, many new communities formed.

In 1599 Franz Xaver von Dietrichstein became Cardinal. With him a radical
counter-reformation began, which led to a systematic extermination of the
Anabaptist movement in Moravia.

Hutterite Community Settlements (1535-1622)

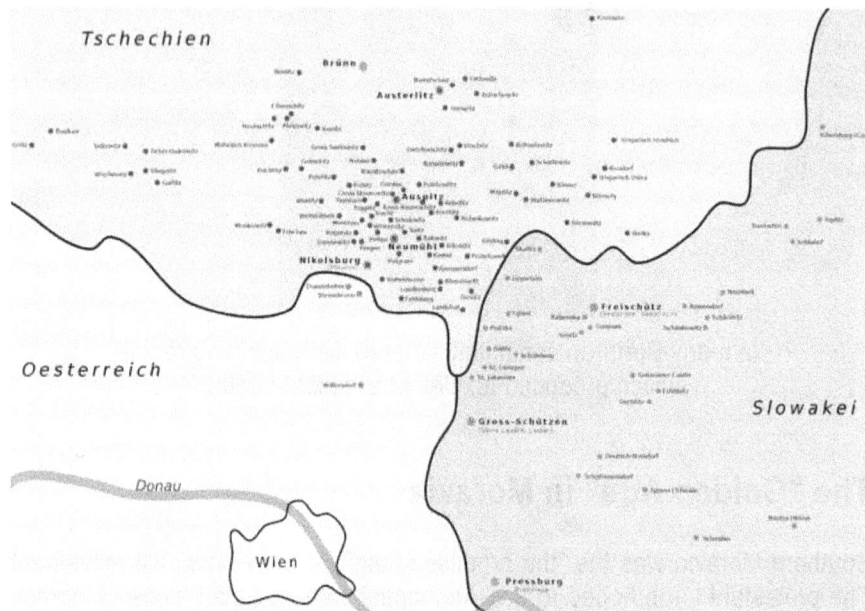

Hutterite Brethren Communities (Haushaben)

Hutterites: Inventors of the Kindergarten and Compulsory Education

Many refugees who arrived in Moravia could neither read nor write. In order to be able to read the Bible, adults became literate. The primary objective was a focus on how to live a God-centered life.

The Hutterite named Peter Walpot (ca. 1518-1578) was an influential educator. He was the first schoolmaster with supervision over approximately 25,000 Hutterites in Moravia and north-eastern Austria.

Among the Hutterites, **compulsory education** was a standard matter 200 years before Maria Theresa.

Scene from the Film "Jakob Hutter and the Hutterites"

Walpots "School Regulations" of 1568 was progressive, described as follows:

- **An orderly kindergarten system**: There were many orphans. The school-based life started with the children from the cradle. Since all women worked, very early on they put their children in the "Klankin-derschuel" (Kindergarten), in which they stayed until they were five.

  Not until 1840, that is, 300 years later, did Friedrich W.A. Fröbel succeed in Germany to implement something similar.

- **Child-oriented pedagogy**: "When a child is brought to school for the first time, his health must be carefully evaluated. If a child has an injury (i.e. an impairment), it should not be hidden. We shouldn't try to break the heads of the little ones who come to school for the first time." In the 16th Century, this adjustment to the needs of the child was an almost revolutionary innovation!

- **Gentle** punishment: It was not allowed to lock children in a dark room. Extreme punishment, such as beating on the head or the mouth, was strictly prohibited. When the rod was necessary, it was to be used with caution and the fear of God. The purpose was to thoroughly instruct the child to recognize the evil of his doings.

- **Hygiene regulations**: Prevention and procedure for dealing with infectious diseases was also developed.

How many of us in the 20th century were brought up quite differently than this!

Coveted Craftsmen

Honesty, hard work, and thriftiness helped Hutterite communities to quickly get into an economic upswing.

Their preferred industries were textiles, pottery, glass making, and metalworking. This made them coveted clock makers, lorimers (those who made horse tack), potters, gardeners, carpenters, and general workmen.

Individual industries complemented each other superbly within each community. This allowed the community to act as "general contractor," able to complete whole coaches or even large projects such as complete mills or breweries.

For example, by 1603 the new mill in Zaina at Stockerau was built "with all accessories." One of many! A complete mill with all the necessary dam sections, and stone- and carpentry-work was no problem for these widely-known mill builders. (See picture)

The Hutterites showed their superiority in "final assembly," where different tradesmen worked together to complete entire contracts themselves

Many had positions of confidence.

Honesty and frugality made the Hutterites especially attractive for administrative posts. Again and again we find them for instance as a cellar master or estate administrator. They were happily entrusted with the noble's brewing and milling operations.

Nobles gladly purchased their products.

Hutterite hand-crafted products were of high quality. Moravian aristocrats were among the customers of the Hutterites. For example, Johann Georg Margrave from Brandenburg employed the Hutterites to build him a coach.

17th century coach, Kutschenmuseum Laa an der Thaya

They did high quality work.

The Hutterites developed extensive rules and quality control standards for their products. Their industries had the character of mass-production and division of labor.

For many products like knives and textiles, the Hutterites were without any local competition. For their ornate knives, ivory had to be procured from far away. Hutterite communities were esteemed as centers of knife production in the 17th century alongside Solinger, Sheffield, and Steyr.

Their doctors had a countrywide reputation for good care.

Kaiser Rudolf II had himself been treated by a Hutterite doctor as well as had Cardinal Dietrichstein, who was the harshest opponent of the group, although he still employed an Anabaptist family doctor.

Pharmacy vessel (reproduction)
in typical haban-ceramic colors on a white background,
signed "Michel Habel 1680"

Problems were not long in coming.

- Guilds and farms were often perceived as unwanted competition

- With affluence came selfishness, which had to be addressed with various rules and ordinances

- Prosperity also attracted "economic refugees" who did not join the communities for reasons of faith; these often caused problems

Trademark "Brüdergeschirr" (Brethren Tableware)

Princes gave it as gifts; nobility and bishops coveted them: the "Brethren Tableware".

It was a trademark and hallmark of Anabaptist folk art!

Even Cardinal Franz Dietrich knew how to value quality. Although he banished all Anabaptists from Moravia in 1622, he still made a large order of this tableware!

Later on, these dishes became known in households everywhere as "holidayware" for special occasions, like weddings. Today, the "Haban cermanics" are common in museums.

Haban pitcher with typical design, 17th century, reproduction.

Typical Haban plate, 1615

Fleeing Anabaptists from Italy brought the secret with them.

The Fayence method of earthenware production was kept a secret among the Hutterites. In order to not be spied on, the kilns were prepared at night. Glaze was also applied at night. Special kilns were the key technology. The potters and jar-makers figured out how to build kilns, in which the flames burned horizontally!

The coveted products were characterized by a white tin glaze background. This was ornamented with brightly-colored paint. White tin oxide, which produces particularly beautiful colors, was extremely expensive. It had to be brought from the Far East.

Centers of Production

- In 17th century **Lower Austria**, family productions arose which produced "Anabaptist" ceramics. These were sold all over south of the Danube.

- **Burgenland** was, at that time, in the hands of Hungarian Protestant princes. After 1622, many Anabaptists lived in what was then western Hungary. Brethern farms existed in Kittsee, Kobersdorf, and Mattersburg. Princes, such as the Batthyánys, had their own Brethren potters.

Mattersburg, former "Krüglerhaus" (house of pottery artisans)

From "Anabaptists Ceramics" to "Gmundner porcelain"

Although the Salzburg Archbishopric ruthlessly persecuted the Anabaptists, their technology was ultimately brought to Salzburg and Gmunden. The "Gmundner pottery" has many similarities with the "Brethren ceramics." Experts suspect that these similarities go back to a direct influence from the

"Anabaptist white potters". In 1719 there was already talk of "Gmundner-Brethren-Anabaptist Tableware."

2004 *Kalinova, Fassbinder-Brückler, Brückler*: Täufer, Hutterer, Habaner

High-Temperature Resistant Enamels

Through Fayence production, high-temperature resistant enamels are laid on the still-unfired glaze coating. The application of decorative painting with a brush requires a skilled artist hand. Correction is impossible.

Broken pieces of a Haban plate, an early Anabaptist ceramic piece, discovered under a house in Steinebrunn, Weinviertel. To the right, examples of enamel powders.

There are only a few colors of metal oxides which do not evaporate at high temperature. The color ranges from ochre yellow or antimony, iron, orange, cobalt blue, copper or chromium oxide green to manganese violet or red.

The high-temperature resistant enamels sink into the glaze while firing at a temperature of about 1,050° C / 1,900° F. In this way, the glaze is especially protected from abrasion and chipping.

The control of the temperature required masterful skill. Anabaptist master craftsmen were probably the first ones to practice this technique in Austria.

Fayence, from the Italian town of Faenza, is a French-derived term for pottery with a porous glaze-body. It is coated with a white or colored tin glaze, usually with high-temperature resistant enamels and fired several times.

Fireproofing: "Made by Hutterites"

Farms, villages, and even whole cities were often victims of major fires. It's no wonder, since most houses had only simple straw roofs. East of the March River, the descendants of the Hutterites, called Habans, developed a revolutionary fire-proof roof.

It's secret for success was as ingenious as it was simple, since it only involved the skillful use of multiple layers of straw and mud!

Unsuccessful fire protection of a different kind:

The Catholic Lord Gundaker von Liechtenstein described which methods were attempted in order to deal with the danger of fire:

In November 1657, he called his son Hartmann, and told him to collect and save all the eggs laid on Maundy Thursday, and to distribute five or six of them to every village for safe keeping, so that if a fire should break out suddenly, an egg could be thrown into the fire. One knows from experience "that by throwing such eggs into the raging inferno, in God's name, the fire will be extinguished."

Lord Hartmann replied with criticism, that this was simply "a superstition and, as far as I can tell, a sin." Furthermore, the said practice was tried out in two fires in Obersulz and Wilfersdorf; they had "an interesting effect, but didn't do anything." His father insisted on the practice.

"Haban roofs" were flame retardant, extinguished fire themselves when they collapsed, increased evacuation time, prevented the spread of fire in villages, were warmer in winter, cooler in summer, were a deterrant to vermin, were more stable in storms, were significantly more durable, and, to top it all off, were cheaper!

It wasn't until the 18th century that many parts of Europe recognized their true value and encouraged their proliferation. But it was too late! The age of brick factories had just begun.

(Adam Landgraf with description of Haban straw roofing)

Graphic from Adam Landgraf with description of Haban straw roofing,
from Pressburg 1772

The Last Hutterite Strongholds in Our Region

East of the March River, just a few villages beyond Niedersulz, lay the Slovak villages of Sobotiste and Velke Levare. These villages (earlier Freischütz and Groß-Schützen) were the last Hutterite strongholds in our region.

In both these villages one can observe how re-catholicization finally won in spite of resistance to it. Only those who fled were not caught by the long arm of the church. The inhabitants of these villages were driven with whips into Jesuit church services as late as 1784. Hutterite leaders were locked in monasteries and un-baptized infants were taken from their parents and placed in orphanages.

In 1782, eleven families managed to flee incognito into Russia to their fellow believers.

About 200 years later, the last remaining were fully assimilated. Even then, the protestant base could not be fully exterminated until World War II.

Haban chapel built in 1763

Catholic Anabaptists (called Habans) were allowed by the Jesuits to keep their common mills, schools, and workshops. There was still a communal monetary fund in 1925.

Haban house, photo from 1965. House has since fallen down

Haban courtyard, photo from around 1965

Velke-Levare = Groß-Schützen:

Vel'ke`Leva're, east of March river. Haban house, house number 86

Descendants of the Hutterites still live today in their old communities. They still have, in part, their same last names. Most know nothing about the Hutterites apart from a few tales. Some have maintained that they were pre-mature communists. The Hutterite straw-clay roofs were replaced just two generations agoInterestingly, with re-catholicization, the quality of workmanship dropped drastically. Today, these Hutterite descendants are mostly simple farmers.

In 1937, American Hutterites visited these communities. Linguistically, they could converse quite well with the older people. But in the area of faith, there was nothing more in common.

(Vgl.: Längin, Bernd G.
Gefangene der Vergangenheit –
Pilger der Gegenwart –
Propheten der Zukunft)

Sung History

Since the earliest days of Christianity, believers have composed and sung songs with great enthusiasm. It is hardly exaggerated to say that no person in history has had so many songs dedicated to him as Jesus Christ.

The Anabaptists were no exception, even though their songs rose out of "complicated circumstances." For example, as 150 Hutterites were held captive in the fortress of Falkenstein north of Vienna, the so-called "Falkenstein Songs" were written. Still today – almost half a millennium later – these songs are sung in German, in part from memory by descendants of those Hutterites.

Martyr-songs are often the stories of the difficult fates of individuals. Because public preaching was banned, they packed their teachings into songs (sung sermons). They are usually joyful songs to the God for whom they have given up everything. They took plenty of time to sing; songs with over 30 verses were no rarity!

The songs were often given a popular melody which everyone already knew, so that everyone could sing along. It seems strange to see the following written over an otherwise serious Martyr-song: "To the tune: There once was a young lady with a jug" or "A flower on the moor." But in just that way, these songs had a strong selling power, since they radiated a defiance of death.

An example of a martyr song:

We roam around in the woods / We're sought after with dogs
We're led like lambs who say nothing / imprisoned and in bonds
We're shown in front of everyone / As if we were insurgents
We are regarded as sheep for slaughter / As heretics and abusers

(Leonhard Schiemer, beheaded in Rattenberg in Tyrol on January 14, 1528)

An example of a sermon-song:

Christ forces no one / to His Glory
Only he is successful / who is ready to want it
Through proper faith and true baptism / works repentance
with a pure heart
He is purchased for heaven.

Felix Mantz, drowned in Zurich January 5, 1527)

Even today the Hutterites do not watch television and other "worldly entertainment;" they love to get together to tell stories and to sing together. Singing as a family each Saturday is a long-standing tradition.

The Language of the Hutterites

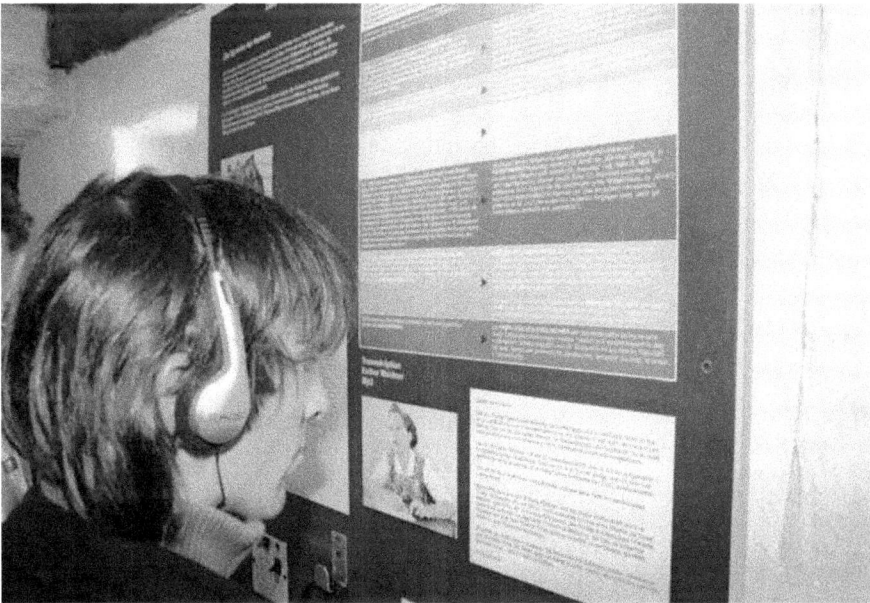

Audio stations give impressions of spoken language.

The oldest Hutterites most likely spoke a south-Tyrol dialect. Later religious refugees from everywhere brought with them the riches of their languages. As a result of the deportation of the "Carinthian Transmigrants" to Transylvania (Romania), Carinthian women became responsible for the rearing of all the small children. Thus, their dialect became the standard for future generations. This mixture of languages formed a unique, unmistakable dialect.

Throughout their journeys through many lands, the Hutterites integrated foreign words into their own language, including terms from Moravia, Slovakia,
Transylvania, and Russia. Today, many words from the English language are
found in their everyday speech.

From the Hutterite Vocabulary

Gmaa(n)	"Gemeinde" (mhd. *gemeine*): 1. Hutterischer Bruderhof 2. Die Kirche der hutterischen Brüder
Bruadr	"Bruder": 1. Der leibliche Bruder 2. Getauftes und somit stimmberechtigtes männliches Mitglied einer hutterischen Gemeinde
Bua	"Bub": unverheirateter männlicher Hutterer über 15 (vgl. *Manndl*)
Manndl	"Männlein": männlicher Hutterer unter 15 (vgl. *Bua*)
Diandl	"Dirnlein": hutterisches Mädchen unter 15; Mehrzahl *Dindle*; (vgl. *Dian*)
Dian	"Dirn": unverheiratete Hutterin über 15; Mehrzahl *Diane*; (vgl. *Diandl*)
Lehr	"Lehre": hutterischer Gottesdienst an Sonn- und Feier-tagen (vgl. *Gebet*)
Gebet	Tägliche hutterische Abendandacht (vgl. *Lehr*)
Åmp	"Amt"; auch *Ampl* "Ämtlein": leitende Funktion, für die man vom Bruderrat "gestimmt" oder "geordnet" wird, vgl. *Schwei(n)mentsch*; *tuts Ampl*
Schwei(n)mentsch	"Schweinemann": Chef der Schweinezucht; ein wichti-ges "lebendiges Amt", für das nur ein verheirateter Bruder gewählt wird; vgl. *Schreindr*
Schreindr	"Schreiner": Chef der hofeigenen Tischlerei; diese Funktion ist ein *tuts Ampl* ("totes Ämtlein"), vgl. *Schwei(n)mentsch*
Diener des Worts	Die alte Bezeichnung für den Prediger

Diener der weltlichen Notdurft	Die alte Bezeichnung für den "Verwalter" bzw. "Mananger"
schtiibln	"stübeln": im Bruderrat tagen und Beschlüsse fassen; nach der alten Bezeichnung "Betstube" für die hutterische Kirche; beim "Stübeln" dürfen nur getaufte Brüder teilnehmen, aber keine Frauen
Zaigbruadr	"Zeugbruder"; dieser "bezeugt" bei Bedarf die im Bruderrat bzw. von der Gemeindeobrigkeit beschlossenen Entscheidungen
Wei(n)zedl	"Weinzedel": verwandt mit "Winzer"; heute auch "farmboss" genannt; teilt die Arbeiten im landwirtschaftlichen Betrieb ein; (in Wien-Nussdorf bedeutete "Weinzedel" Vorarbeiter in einem Weinhauerbetrieb)
Ankela	Großmutter: eine Wortbildung zu "Ahne"; das Wort kam ursprünglich ausschließlich in Kärnten vor; vgl. *Klana-Schual-Ankela*
Klana-Schual-Ankela	Kindergartentante; auch diese Funktion ist ein hutterisches "Amt"; vgl. *Ámp, Ankela, Klana Schual*
gschtimmp	"gestimmt": vom Plenum der getauften Brüder (Bruderrat) in eine Funktion gewählt, vgl. *Ámp, gurnt*
gurnt	"geordnet": von der Gemeindeführung (Prediger, Verwalter, *Weinzedel, Zaigbruadr*) ohne Einberufung des Bruderrates für eine Funktion bestimmt; vgl. *gschtimmp*
Seeln	"Seelen": Mitglieder einer Gemeinde
Leicht	"Leiche": Begräbnis
Wåcht	Totenwache: an ihr nehmen mehrere Prediger und hunderte Hutterer aus vielen Gemeinden teil
Sorgela	"Sorgelein": unverheiratetes hutterisches Mädchen, das einer jungen Mutter für das Kind "sorgen" hilft
Daitscha Schual	"Deutsche Schule": die Konfessionsschule der Hutterer; täglich eine Stunde vor und eine Stunde nach dem englischsprachigen Regelunterricht in der hofeigenen Schule; hier wird in den meisten Gemeinden noch immer die Kurrentschrift verwendet
Schmiednlait	"Schmiedeleute": der Schmied Michael Waldner kehrte 1859 in Russland als Erster wieder zur Gütergemein-

	schaft zurück; vg. *Dårreslait, Lehrerlait*
Dårreslait	"Dariusleute": die Gruppe von Darius Walter kehrt bald nach den "Schmiedeleuten" zur Gütergemeinschaft zurück; vgl. *Schmiednlait, Lehrerlait*
Lehrerlait	"Lehrerleute": nach dem Lehrer Jakob Wipf, der in Russland ein mennonitisches Lehrerseminar besucht hat; er verlässt Russland mit seiner Gruppe drei Jahre später als die übrigen Hutterer; vgl. *Schmiednlait, Dårreslait*
Klei(n)serlait	"Kleinsasserleute": die besonders fortschrittliche Gruppe von Jacob Kleinsasser, die sich 1992 von den konservativeren Schmiedeleuten in Manitoba abgespaltet hat
dees	"ihr" (s. Textzeile 22): ein germanisches Reliktwort, das sich im Bairischen erhalten konnte; als "ees" heute auch noch im Wienerischen bekannt; vgl. *enk*
enk	"euch" (s. Textzeile 22): ein germanisches Reliktwort, das sich im Bairischen erhalten konnte; als "eng" heute auch noch im Wienerischen bekannt; vgl. *dees*
lätich	Dienstag "Ergetag": zum griechisch-arianischen Theologen "Arius"; ein ursprünglich gotisches Lehnwort, das über die Langobarden ins Bairische gelangte; vgl. *Pfingstich, Pfaat*
Pfingstich	"Pfingsttag": zu griechisch *pempte* "der fünfte" Tag (vom Sonntag an gezählt); ein ursprünglich gotisches Lehnwort, das über die Langobarden ins Bairische gelangte; vgl. *lätich, Pfaat*
Pfaat	Hemd: zu griechisch *paidos* "Messgewand"; ein ursprünglich gotisches Lehnwort, das über die Langobarden ins Bairische gelangte; vgl. *Pfingstich, lätich*
Álmr	"Almer": Bücherschrank (des Predigers); zu lateinisch *armarium* "Schrank"; das Wort war früher auch in Kärnten und Südtirol verbreitet
Nåchpling	Abendessen: eine lautliche Entstellung von "Nachtmahl"; in ähnlicher Lautform auch in Kärnten
Schtranggl	"Strankelein": grüne Bohnen; ein besonders in Kärnten gebräuchliches slawisches Lehnwort

mit seen redn	mit ihnen reden: "seen" ist eine in Kärnten übliche Deklinationsform des Pronomens „sie"
Tschichtl	"Geschichtlein": Erzählung, Märchen; die Assimilation im Anlaut ist für das Hutterische typisch; ähnlich auch *tsågg* "gesagt", *tsungen* "gesungen" oder *pfrågg* "gefragt"
zu die Lait khumme(n)	"Zu den Leuten kommen": mit dem 15. Geburtstag beendet man die *Daitscha Schual* und verlässt auch die *Essns-Schual*; man isst ab jetzt mit den Erwachsenen und wird vom *Wei(n)zedl* zur Arbeit eingeteilt
Essns-Schual	"Essens-Schule": Kinderspeisesaal; Kinder bis 15 nehmen ihre Mahlzeiten getrennt von den Erwachsenen ein; sie werden vom Lehrer der *Daitscha Schual* und dessen Frau betreut; in konservativen Gemeinden ist auch hier eine nach Geschlechtern getrennte Sitzordnung wie in der "Ess-Stube" der Erwachsenen vorgeschrieben
Heeb-Ankela	Hebamme: heute aber gehen die Huttererinnen zur Entbindung in ein Krankenhaus; vgl. *Ankela*
enta	bevor, früher (s. Textzeile 17): im Südbairischen entstanden aus "ehender"
featn	"ferten": voriges Jahr; eine im Bairischen häufige Wortbildung zu "fern"; bei den Dariusleuten *fäätn*
taitsch guat	"deutsch gut": besonders gut; Steigerungsadverb bei den Schmiedeleuten; bei den Dariusleuten stattdessen *schermánt guat*, bei den Lehrerleuten *gschmååch guat*
schermánt guat	"charmant gut": besonders gut; Steigerungsadverb bei den Dariusleuten; bei den Schmiedeleuten stattdessen *taitsch guat*, bei den Lehrerleuten *gschmååch guat*
gschmååch guat	"geschmach gut": besonders gut; Steigerungsadverb bei den Lehrerleuten; bei den Schmiedeleuten stattdessen *taitsch guat*, bei den Dariusleuten *schermánt guat*
Schlååen	"Schlappen": das übliche Wort für Hausschuhe bei den Schmiedeleuten; bei den Dariusleuten *Schlippr*, bei den Lehrerleuten *Pintsch*
Schlippr	"Slipper" (aus dem Englischen): das übliche Wort für Hausschuhe bei den Dariusleuten; bei den Schmiedeleuten *Schlååen*, bei den Lehrerleuten *Pintsch*
Pintsch	das übliche Wort für Hausschuhe bei den Dariusleu-

	ten; bei den Schmiedeleuten *Schlååen*, bei den Dariusleuten *Schlippr*
Schnea	"Schnee": die Diphthongierung des alten /ê/ und /œ/ ist südbairisch, wie z.B. auch in *geahn* "gehen", s. Textzeile 11) oder *peas* "böse"; so nur bei den Schmiedeleuten; bei den Darius- und Lehrerleuten hört man hingegen *Schnee* und *pees*
Dr peasa Feind	"Der böse Feind": Teufel, Versucher; zur Lautform *peas* für "böse" bei den Schmiedeleuten s. *Schnea*
Schtruu	"Stroh" (s. Textzeile 25): die o-Laute sind bei den Huttern in ihrer südmährischen Zeit zu *u* geworden, so auch in *gruuß* "groß" (Textzeile 22), *huuch* "hoch", *Uste* "Ostern", *hupsn* "hopsen" usw.
Hupskhruut	"Hopskrote" (Hopskröte): für ein lebhaftes Kleinkind; zu den u-Lauten s. *Schtruu*
Schturrela	ein kleines Kaufhaus: zum englischen Wort *store* "Geschäft"; zum hutterischen [u] in diesem Wort vgl. *Schtruu*
Khombain	Mähdrescher: aus dem englischen *combine (harvester)*
I(n)schain	Traktor: aus dem englischen *engine* (Motor; Lokomotive)
glaichn	mögen, z.B. *Ich glaich Schmånd* (Ich mag Rahm): möglicherweise eine Lehnprägung nach dem englischen *to like* (mögen), doch gibt es auch ein mhd. *gelîchen* mit ähnlicher Bedeutung
Prärielait	"Prärieleute": von den mehr als 1.200 aus Südrussland in die USA ausgewanderten Hutterern gründeten 400 drei Bruderhöfe in South Dakota; die übrigen siedelten in der "Prärie" von SD im Privateigentum; vgl. *Schmiednlait*

The previous linguistical section from pages 84 to 88 was prepared and supplied by Dr. Wilfried Schabus of Vienna.

Transcription of an Audio Recording from Esther Waldner

The audio stations in the Anabaptist museum offer impressive examples of the language of the Hutterites. Esther Waldner lives in a Hutterite colony in Tasmania, Australia.

Griass dich, Elmar!

Mia do i Rocky Cape Gmaa sa(n) fru zu vu dia hean, und zu mit Leidn hobn zu toa vu di Lända do wu unsra Vorväta härkumme. Es 's scho(?) viel Joa'n won unsra Leit sein as Tirol gonge, und späta Mähren, vu Siebenbürgen und Russlondt. Vu do duet sein se härkumme noch Amerika in 1877. ochtzehnhundertsiebmundsiebzich

Ich bin de Esther Waldner. Ich bin 22 zwaundzwnazich Joa olt. Ich bin aufgwochsn i e huttrischa Gmaa i Süddakota. Duet bin ich in di Schuel gonge, und ich hob duet gwohnt bis ich bi umgezogn zu e ondra Gmaa in Minnesota i 2003. zwatausnddrei

Hitz bin ich do in Australien i maa Brueder und saa Weib helfn mit sendra zwaa klaana Kinda.

Meine Eltr, da David und di Berta Waldner, und ma jingris Gschwistrich wont i e Gmaa i Süddakota. Kro vor ich bin noch Australien kumme is ma Olvetta, da David Waldner, gschtorbn. Ich bi ba de Leicht gwesn. Ma Olvetta is aufgwochsn i Kanada, wons si sin aufkrisen ("aufgerissen"?) durch di Weltkrieg. Sei Vota, da Johannes Waldner, hot in de Bon Homme Gmaa glebt in Amerika, un sei Olvetta, da Michl Waldner, is vu Russlondt kumme(n).

Di Gmaa do i Australien is a klaana. Die Moonsleit tue mit Eisen orbiten, schwaasen, und Schmidtn-Orbe. De Weibr sorgn de Kindr, kuuchn, naane, wooschn und varrichtn. Ma eesn zomm, und ich helf i di Schuel.

Gott sei mit dir.

Rooms D + E

Path of Suffering and Persecution – Above All in the Region of Today's Lower Austria

View of room D

The Anabaptist Mandate from Speyer

This mandate, also called "Constitution," is a collection of regulations which were formed in 1529 at the Diet of Speyer. The following are its main points:

Whoever is re-baptized shall be punished by death – without a trial through an inquisitional court

Whoever disallows his newborn children to be baptized shall be punished by death

Anabaptists, who have escaped to other territories, shall be punished where they are

With this mandate all local regulations in the entire empire were made the same.

Burning at the Stake, Drowning, or Beheading?
Fire, Water, or Sword

The city council of Zurich decided the following on March 7, 1526:

> *"Therefore we now give the named men an earnest law, dictating and warning, that whether in the city or in areas further out, no men, women, or girls are allowed to baptize others. Whoever would further do so may be taken by our men and, after their conviction, be drowned without grace."*

In 1527, Archduke Ferdinand I adopted this mandate for the Austrian Empire.

In 1528, the Habsburg Emperor Charles V adopted a tough regulation against the Anabaptists, outlawing all of them in the entire empire.

There was almost no place in Europe where the Anabaptist faith could live freely.

They had the whole Catholic Habsburg Empire and the Swiss Reformers against them. Even in most of the Lutheran areas they were persecuted and killed.

The Chronicles of Hutterites reads in places like a report from the front, in which the latest deaths were reported:

"In Vienna, 23 and many secretly convicted. In Neustadt, 4. Grätzenstein (Kreuzenstein), 6. Melk, 3. Grein, 1. Lembach, 45. Mödling, 4. Pöggstal, 1. Ybbs, 1. Krems, 1. Böheimkirchen, 2. Ottental, 4. Putteshofen, 4. Veldsberg, 1. Falkenstein, 5..."

However, the persecution played a significant role in the rapid spread of the movement. The courage with which the believers went to their death attracted more followers.

Within a few years, the whole southern German region was involved. After the first five years, nearly all influential peoples from the beginning days were arrested, interrogated, tortured and executed including Jörg Blaurock in Tyrol, Balthasar Hubmaier in Vienna, Hans Hut in Augsburg, and Jakob Hutter in Innsbruck.

Mass burning of 18 Anabaptists in Salzburg.
Copper engraving from the Märtyrerspiegel
(Martyr's mirror) by Luiken.

Stretched on the Rack

A confession from the mouth of the accused was required for a conviction, introduced by the Romans as an inalienable right. To this end, the accused was often "embarrassingly questioned" (by torture). This was precisely regulated. Often just the sight of the torture equipment was enough to get the necessary confession.
Thousands of Anabaptists in Europe in the 16th and 17th centuries were tortured using ropes and weights which stretched the whole body which then was seared with glowing tongs.
The main purpose of punishment was to elicite fear. Executions were nasty but celebratory public ceremonies. Because of their stead-fastness, Anabaptists were less and less often executed in public. The authorities feared an adverse effect on the population.

Torture rack in ladder form, Schloss Greillen-stein / Waldviertel

The Disaster in Münster –
Now there was a scapegoat.

The Anabaptist movement in our history books is shrouded with deep silence. One exception, however, is almost always given a lot of room, that is, the short reign of the "Fanatic of Münster." It's no wonder, since these extreme and violent events from 1535 are "ready for Hollywood." Artists, too, have taken up this well-marketable topic of the "Anabaptists of Münster."

In the 16th century, there was a general mode of thought that the end of the world was near. Fanatics from every nation flocked to Münster, because that city should become the "New Jerusalem" and the whole globe be ruled from the city. John of Leyden had himself anointed as the King of God's People. Subsequently, Münster was besieged for nearly a year and a half by Catholic and Protestant troops. Extreme situations developed, polygamy was rampant, and the unruly were quickly tried in court. People held fanatically to the hope of a quick victory. Starvation set in. Soon the slogan was issued: God could make bread from stones! Half-starved people bit into stones in faith which soon ended in disillusionment as death came to many. Finally, the city fell. The "king" and two of its leaders were tortured in the town square with red-hot tongs until they died. Even today you can see iron cages in which their bodies were hung in display from the façade of the Lambert church in Münster.

For the enemies of the Anabaptists, this incident was very welcome. Now a new wave of persecution came upon many.

Münster is in no way, however, representative of the Anabaptist movement. In 1699, the Lutheran church historian Gottfried Arnold wrote in his "History of the Church and Heretics":

> *"But it is clear from so many documents that the other Anabaptists took no part in this, but had an outrage and disgust for all that took place. They have for these things only the highest disapproval and condemnation."*

For the Hutterites these events were *"an atrocity that the devil had erected."*

Why were the Anabaptists persecuted so relentlessly?

Besides the Catholic Church, the Protestants were also involved in it. Protestant leaders including Zwingli and Luther also took part in this, albeit with less intensity.

Most likely, several contributing factors came together to bring this about:

- The authorities had a panicking fear of the political and social consequences, should Anabaptist ideals be implemented (such as eradicating the extreme differences between classes of people and the ranks in the church).

- The memories of Michael Gaismair and Thomas Müntzer were still fresh, whose peasant uprisings seemed to be a floating "spectre" in the area. (Similar fears were triggered by the fanatics of Münster).

- There was also the rationally unexplainable disgust for coexistence with the unbaptized, which were regarded as devils.

- Later there was envy and mistrust regarding the economic superiority and efficiency of the Anabaptists.

Dissidents have always had it hard!

The Reformation in Austria

By 1520, large parts of the population in Austria were engaged in the Reformation. Up to 90% had turned to the new doctrine.

In Tyrol, approximately 20,000 people were Anabaptists. By 1531, there had already been about 1,000 executions!

Under the strict rule of Ferdinand I, a massive defense against the Reformation was affected.

The Anabaptists were punished with death. But these measures showed no effect. Their courage birthed more followers. It is estimated that about 4,000 people lost their lives.

The Successful Counter-Reformation

Mainly in the period from 1565 to 1618, the re-catholicizing of largely Protestant Austria succeeded. The Protestant pastors were gradually expelled. The "Reformation Commission" went throughout the country and used violence against any resistance. Under Ferdinand II, the last phase of the re-catholicization was put in place. From this period comes the saying "make someone Catholic," which is still commonly used in modern German.

At the beginning of the 30 Years' War (1618-1648), the Protestant aristocracy united with their Bohemian counterparts against Emperor Ferdinand II. After their devastating defeat of 1620 at the Battle of White Mountain near Prague, Ferdinand had a free hand to completely restore a Catholic country. Under Archbishop Firmian, the Edict of Expulsion of 1731 was adopted, which led to the emigration of 22,000 out of Salzburg.

The result of the Counter-Reformation was a country with a largely unified religion, the price of which was very high. Besides great human suffering, some sensitive sectors of the economy were affected, so that economic slumps occurred.

Empress Maria Theresa required forced emigration of all "non-Catholics," banishing many to Hungary and Transylvania, Anabaptists and Protestants being secretly arrested, deported, and re-educated.

Josef II was a child of the Enlightenment and implemented radical reforms. With the "Edict of Tolerance" of 1781, Josef II secured religious freedom for

Lutherans, Calvinists, and the Greek-Orthodox. This freedom, however, was not granted to the Anabaptists.

"With the Concordat of 1855, the Catholic faith became, unofficially but in reality, the state religion and the Catholic church the state church or at least raised to the state-supporting church."

With the Protestant Edict of 1861 Emperor Franz Joseph I, the Protestant faiths (Augburg and Helvetic Confessions) were granted religious equality. At this point the hurtful designation of "non-Catholic" was taken away.

Thousands move away secretly: On to Moravia – or each save himself, who can!

Everywhere "heretics" were hunted. In Austria alone more than 1,000 men and women were executed. Between Tyrol and the Enns River there was hardly any way to survive.

But where should they flee?

The northern margraviate of Moravia became, at that time, a region of tolerance. The mostly Protestant lords became protectors of the Anabaptists.

In Tyrol, Jakob Hutter quickly realized that his spiritual brothers were hunted everywhere and were finding it impossible to survive. He launched an astonishing project for his time:

The secret departure of thousands of Anabaptists to Moravia!!

Despite persecution, the Anabaptist faith had many followers until the late 16th century. Missionaries regularly visited the region in order to win new friends in faith and to encourage already existing communities. They held meetings in hidden, remote places. Those who decided to emigrate were gathered together. Along the escape routes, empty cabins served as supply depots: organized, outfitted with bread, ham, and other staples. Decisive mountain passes and bridges were watched by the government around the clock. In larger groups they went by foot in the direction of Inn. They went further by ship on the Inn and Danube Rivers to Grafenwörth bei Krems. There helpers awaited them, who led them across the land through the Weinviertel to the northern Hutterite settlements.

Child sitting on anvil

The strongest in a group (including young smiths) of those fleeing over the mountains and rivers carried a bulk of the load in order to support the physically weak.

In Krems' Surroundings, Helpers for Refugees Waited at the Ready.

They tried to help their brothers and sisters in faith across land through the Weinviertel to the northern Hutterite settlements. Anabaptists from other parts of Austria and Europe tried to reach this "Promised Land," too, attempting to reach Moravia. Some escape attempts ended on the flames of a pyre.

An escape gathering point. Scene from a film by Luis Holzer and Taura Films about the life of Jakob Hutter.

Jakob Hutter († 1536)
The Great Organizer from Puster Valley

The "Hutterite Brethren" were named after him. As a strong leader Hutter brought a new level of organization to the community in Moravia, where their social and spiritual life got back on track. This ensured its survival until today.

As persecution in his home region of Tyrol steadily increased, Hutter organized small groups that should escape to Moravia. The Anabaptists there were treated with tolerance. He still remained in the Alps for some time and attended those left behind.

In 1531, he was called to arbitrate a dispute in Austerlitz (Moravia). There he founded a Brethren community of Christian settlements. From 1535 on, the number of Anabaptist refugees steadily grew in massive proportions in Moravia, which led to them being more and more harassed.

Jakob Hutter had to flee. When at midnight he asked at a house if he could come in and warm up a bit, he was seized. He was immediately brought to Innsbruck. There it was attempted to force him to recant his faith using terrible torture, but without success.

Jacob Hutter was burned at the stake in front of the Goldenes Dachl (Golden Roof) in Innsbruck at the end of February 1536. It is said by the Hutterites that even Ferdinand I should have been able to see the flames from his residence.

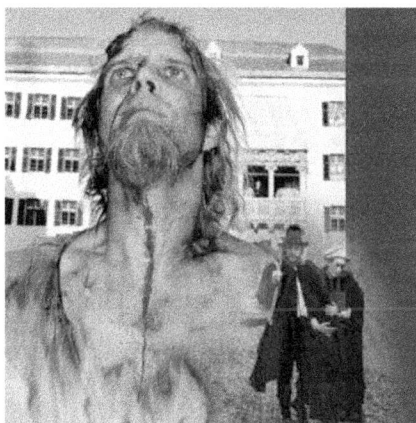

Burning of Jakob Hutter in Taura-Films "Jakob Hutter and the Hutterites" played by actor Florian Adamski.

The Hutterite "Geschichtbuch" (Book of History) reports of those who were
sentenced to death:

*The Hutterite "Geschichtbuch" reports the death of those condemned: "As
priests from their evil and revenge-filled zeal, they wanted to drive the
devil out of him [Jacob Hutter], so they left him in ice-cold water and then
lead him into a warm room, beating him with rods. After having wounded
his body, they poured brandy into his wounds, lit them on fire, and let him
burn. They tied his hands and put a gag in his mouth, that he might not
reveal to them their wickedness. They put a plumed hat on him and carried him into the house of their idols, playing with all sorts of stupidity and
tomfoolery with him. And since he persevered steadily and honestly as a
Christian hero in his faith, he was condemned by the children of Caiaphas
and Pilate, being carried out alive to the stake and burned. He was above
the level of many people and his fidelity was seen."[1]*

(Wolkan, R. (Hg.), Das große Geschichtsbuch der Hutterischen Brüder;
Bautz, W., Jakob Hutter. In: Biographisches-Bibliographisches
Kirchenlexikon. Bd. II.)

In 2007 a Hutterite delegation
visited the location of Jakob
Hutter's burning in Innsbruck
and viewed the memorial
plaque at that location

---

[1] „Da vermeinten die Pfaffen aus ihrem bösen, rachgierigen Eifer, sie wollten den Teufel
aus ihm [Jakob Hutter] bannen, ließen ihn in ein eiskaltes Wasser setzen und nach dem
in ein warme Stuben führen, mit Ruten schlagen. Auch habens ihm seinen Leib verwundt,
Branntwein in die Wunden gossen, an ihm angezündet und brennen lassen. Sie bunden
ihm die Händ, auch wiederum einen Knebel ins Maul, auf daß er ihnen ihr Schalkheit
nicht konnt anzeigen oder offenbaren. Sie setzten ihm auch ein Hut mit einem Federbu-
schen auf, führten ihn ins Haus ihrer Götzen, hatten auf allerlei Weis ihr Narren- und
Affenspiel mit ihm. Da er aber beständig und redlich als ein christlicher Held in seim
Glauben verharret, ward er nach viel erduldter Tyrannei von den argen Kaiphas- und
Pilatuskindern verurteilet, also lebendig in Scheiterhaufen getan und verbrannt. Dabei
über die Maß viel Volks gewesen ist und sein Redlichkeit gesehen."

The Fate of the "Corner Preachers": Emissaries Sent as far as Constantinople

"That God's Word and will be made known to the people."

(Gran, Codex III 155, Blat 353)

By their enemies they were called malicious "corner preachers."
The emissaries of the Hutterites were mostly those who

"like night owls and ravens swing through the countryside, as they could not allow themselves to be seen by day". (GGB p.187)

(Wolkan, Rudolf, Hg., Das große Geschicht-Buch der Hutterischen Brüder*)*

They travelled by foot through forests and mountains and preached at night. They mostly stayed only in secret "corners" in order to share the message of salvation. Whether in the silence of forests, in mills, on remote farms, or in pig stalls, they testified of Jesus, even at public executions.

Poland, Galicia, Hungary, Italy, even Thessalonica and Constantinople were their goals. In accordance with Jesus' mission, the Hutterite missionaries were sent out in all directions two by two. Each one had letters and pamphlets in his pockets. The local community supported them through prayers and encouraging letters

Their ministry was seldom in vain. Wherever they preached, people changed their lives and created Christian communities. *"There was a time when nearly all of Tyrol and Styria thought like the Anabaptists."* (*Loserth, Johann,* in: Mennonitisches Lexikon)

"Corner Preacher"from the film by Holzer.

These emissaries took full joy in continuing on. A few of them, however, indulged themselves by surviving and returning.

The Mice Carried away His Toes!
Held in Stocks in Eggenburg

Peter Voit was an Anabaptist missionary and a close colleague of Jakob Hutter. He was caught in Eggenburg. Both his legs were "clamped in stocks," so that his feet began to rot. In this helpless condition, he had to watch as the mice *"carried away his toes before his very eyes."*

Later freed, he was taken in by Moravian Anabaptists. They were in terrible circumstances in 1538 and had to live on the open fields. There he eventually had to have both legs amputated. Nevertheless, "after such a long time of life," he died in 1570.

Ziegelschmidt, A.J.F. Die Älteste Chronik der Hutterischen Brüder (The Oldest
Chronicle of the Hutterite Brethren)

Hans Hut (ca.1490-1527)
Itinerant Preacher Successful in Austrian Lands

Among the Anabaptists, Hans Hut was the most fiery of preachers and "soul winners." His preaching style was characterized as apocalyptic. This bookseller and distributor of pamphlets is responsible for winning more followers in two years than all other Anabaptist leaders put together. He left deep footprints, especially in Austria.

After he met Hubmaier in Nikolsburg in 1526 he had to flee, staying for two weeks in the Kärntner Street in Vienna, where he baptized 50 people. He soon moved on to Melk and Steyr, where he was arrested. He successfully escaped. He then went to Freistadt, Gallneukirchen, Linz, and Passau. Wherever he went, he always left numerous baptized people behind. He finally came to Augsburg via Schärding, Braunau, Laufen, and Salzburg. This would be the last stop for this father of five.

Hans Hut

The following reports how his life ended:

Hut was left to die in his cell after being tortured thirteen times. A candle left by one of the torturers ignited the straw in his cell. The smoke took the last of his strength from him and caused him to asphyxiate. As though that were not enough, he was tried as a heretic after his death.

His body was publicly burned after his conviction on December 7, 1527.

That which Hans Hut declared before his inquisitors he also lived out:

"One must sincerely repent, then believe and be baptized."

In his teaching to each person baptized, he connected baptism with the duty to obey God's word with one's life.

(Ein Sendbrief Johannes Hutten, Brünn; *Bautz, F.W.*, Hans Hut. In: Biographisches-Bibliographisches Kirchenlexikon. *Bd. II)*

That is Why They Risked Their Lives: The Message of the "Corner Preachers"

The missionaries of the Anabaptists were convinced that the only way one could recognize his sinfulness was through God's Word, which could lead one to repentance.

"They are free without dread
giving witness of the truth,
That Jesus Christ is the truth,
the way, and also the life."

(Leonhard Schiemer, former Barefoot Monk, converted to the Anabaptists and, in 1528, beheaded in Vienna).

"We believe in Jesus Christ,
that in Him is all our redemption and our salvation.
...though many are screaming against us,
that we should attempt to become godly through our own deeds,
but to that, however, we say 'no'."

Peter Riedemann, 9 years in jail, Rechenschaft, p. 291)

The Feared Hunter of Anabaptists, Dietrich von Hartitsch: Hunting down People in Lower Austria

Dietrich von Hartitsch was something like the chief of a special task force. The royal mandate against the Anabaptists of 1527 was in his saddle bag. The hatred of all these Anabaptists was in his heart. Ferdinand I wanted to finally be done with these "heretics." Dietrich and his 20 horses (riders) were sufficient. They used "short legal proceedings." Anyone who was loosely associated with Anabaptism could be executed immediately, simply hung on the nearest city gate posts, for example. Whoever housed an Anabaptist would have his house destroyed. Nobody can say how many there were who fell into the cruel hands of Dietrich von Hartitsch. In Neulengbach there were at least 18. (His accomplice Berthold Aichele made it into another area in order to kill 40 missionaries and 1,200 heretics). A blossoming spiritual renewal movement in Lower Austria came in this way to a standstill.

Mennonite Encyclopaedia Vol.2, p.258; baptism of fire, Peter Hoover, p.218

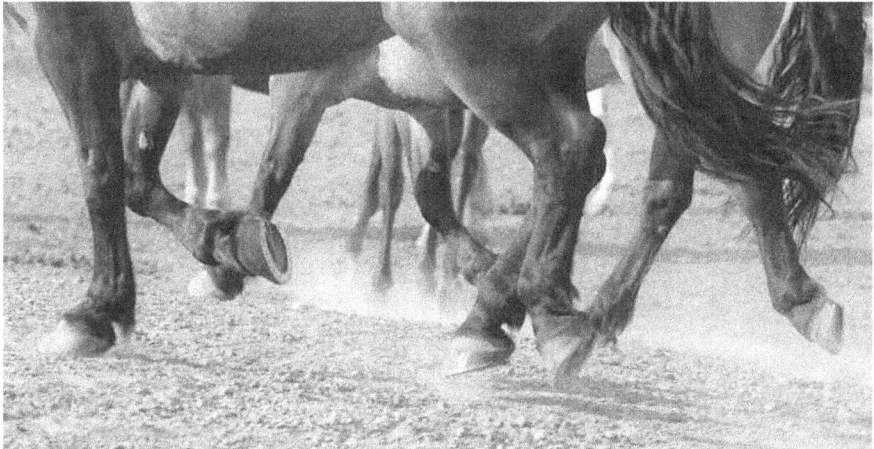

Hartitsch was broadly feared by the Anabaptists throughout the region of today's Lower Austria

Successful Re-Catholicization

Primarily in the years between 1565 and 1618, the re-catholicization of broadly Protestant Austria occurred. The "Reformation Commission" went throughout the country and used violence against any resistance. Under Ferdinand II, the last phase of the re-catholicization was put in place. From this period comes the idiom "make someone Catholic," which is still commonly used in modern German.

At the beginning of the 30 Years' War (1618-1648), the Protestant aristocracy united with their Bohemian counterparts against Emperor Ferdinand II. After their devastating defeat of 1620 at the Battle of White Mountain near Prague, Ferdinand had a free hand to completely restore a Catholic country.

One hundred years later, this religious "cleansing" gradually came to an end.

Empress Maria Theresa required forced emigration of all "non-Catholics," banishing many to Hungary and Transylvania, the Anabaptists and Protestants being secretly arrested, deported, or re-educated.

The result of the Counter-Reformation was a country with a largely unified religion, the price of which was very high. Besides great human suffering, some sensitive sectors of the economy were affected, so that economic slumps occurred.

From 1579, Olmützer Bishop Franz von Dietrichstein was responsible for the expulsion of the Anabaptists. Copper engraving by Ä. Sadtler 1604

⇨

In the 16th century, the Anabaptist movement was heavily represented throughout Austria. Map of Austria with locations where Anabaptists are mentioned to have been.

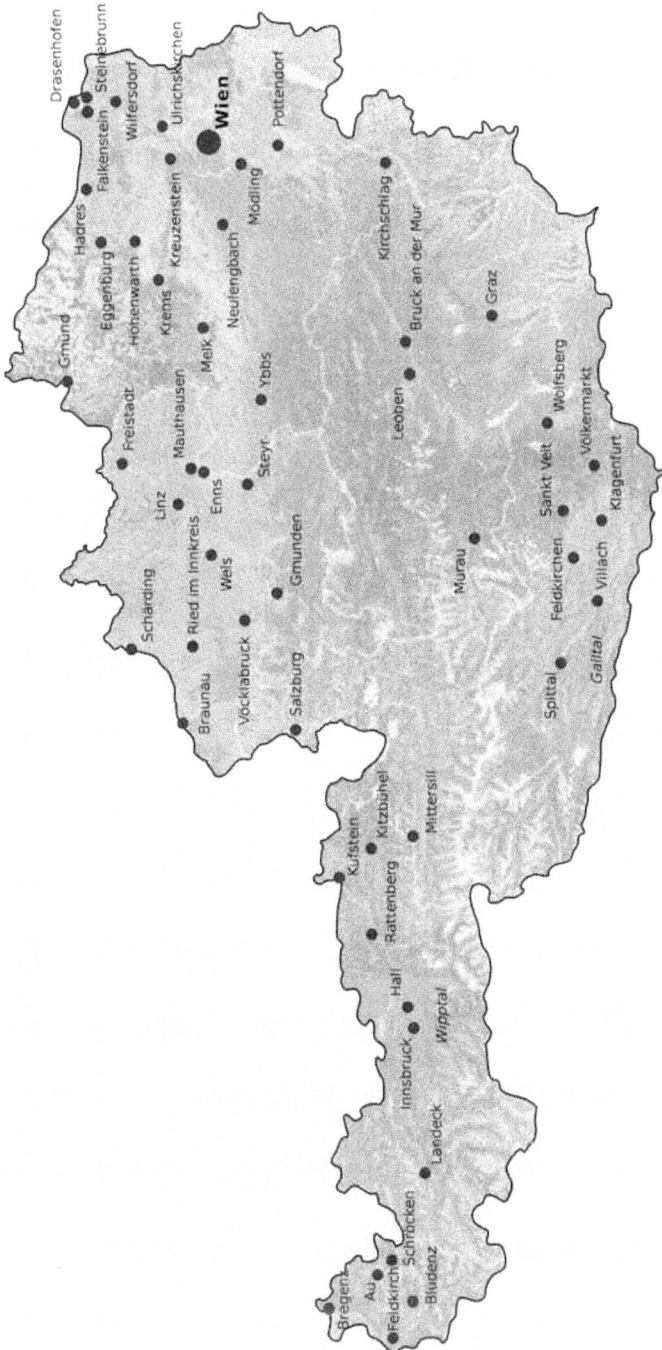

Drasenhofen
Steinebrunn
Falkenstein
Ulrichskirchen
Wilfersdorf
Wien
Pottendorf
Haares
Eggenburg
Kreuzenstein
Mödling
Hohenwarth
Krems
Neulengbach
Kirchschlag
Gmünd
Melk
Bruck an der Mur
Freistadt
Ybbs
Graz
Mauthausen
Steyr
Linz
Enns
Leoben
Wolfsberg
Scharding
Ried im Innkreis
Gmunden
Sankt Veit
Völkermarkt
Wels
Klagenfurt
Braunau
Vöcklabruck
Murau
Feldkirchen
Villach
Salzburg
Spital
Gailtal
Kitzbühel
Mittersill
Kufstein
Rattenberg
Hall
Wipptal
Innsbruck
Landeck
Schröcken
Bregenz
Au
Feldkirch
Bludenz

From the Weinviertel to the Galleys!
The Assault on Steinebrunn

The lovely place of Steinebrunn in the northern Weinviertel was the scene of a moving story on the night of December 6, 1539. Royal soldiers assaulted a "Brethren Farm" and led away about 150 Anabaptists as captives to the castle Falkenstein. Women and children were released and the men, 90 in number, were held prisoner.

After eight days, the marshal of King Ferdinand arrived with a member of clergy and an executioner. He demanded information about their Anabaptist faith and where their wealth was stored.

> *"Then they unanimously confessed that Christ their Savior alone would be their comfort, hope, and even dearest treasure, refuge, and best part, because of whom they received from the Father love and grace."*

(Das große Geschichtsbuch d. Hutterischen Brüder, 159)

From the fortress, the deportation of Anabaptists en route to galley ships could be watched for long into the distance

From letters that the prisoners smuggled from the castle it is known that these men figured that they would be executed as martyrs with great anguish.

Five weeks later the marshal came back from Vienna with horsemen. He demanded that the Anabaptists recant their beliefs. Whoever remained in his faith would be delivered to the imperial admiral Andreas Doria. Each would have to live the rest of his life as a Galley slave on warships at the oars, rowing in the battle against the Turks.

Ninety men, mostly family fathers, were bound in chains in pairs. The prisoners were taken first to Kagran, then to Vienna, and on to Trieste via Semmering.

Religious comrades followed their brothers and reported their fates to their families. After arriving in Trieste, an escape attempt succeeded in the sixth night of captivity. They all managed to escape over the city wall. Twelve of them were recaptured the next day, from which no one heard anything ever again.

But 68 brothers happily returned to their community.

Galley ship, 15th century. The likelihood that their lives would end on board ship was very high for the captives.

Even the Second in Command to the King Couldn't Hold back His Tears

The parting of the Brethren from their loved ones was a very shocking incident and the "Martyr's Mirror" reported this as follows:

"After that they said their farewells with warm tears and crying eyes, affectionately reminding each other that they should hold to the Lord and their recognized truth firmly and steadfastly, one of the others commending them too, many times, to the watch-care of God without knowing if they would ever see each other alive again. Thus, husband and wife had to separate and leave their young children, which no flesh and blood could have done, if not through the power of God and for His sake.

This farewell was so heart-rending that even the King's field commander and his men couldn't hold back their tears. But their sisters had to stay in the palace and see the many Brethren's signs and heartache, as long as they could see them over the wall."

(Tieleman Jansz van Braght, Märyrerspiegel; Erstausgabe 1660)

Dutch were Encouraged by the People of Steinebrunn 350 years ago.

The Martyr's Mirror

Original German title translates as follows: "The bloodly setting or martyrs' mirror of baptistic and defenseless Christians who have suffered for their testimony of Jesus who is their source of all joy, and have been killed since the time of Christ until the year 1660."

The "Martyrs Mirror," a 10 cm thick, leather-bound, heavy book, now belongs to the Christian classics. It has a special vibrancy with its copperplates.

The most important edition is that of Dutchman Tieleman Jansz van Braghts from the year 1660.

Jan Luiken contributed to the 2nd edition in 1685, now famous for its engravings. Monks in Pennsylvania, USA worked on the first German edition from 1748-1750.

Interesting detail:

The "Steinebrunn-Falkenstein-Martyrs of 1539" are particularly emphasized by one of the engravings. Today, many people from all over the world know this name because of the engraving.

Please note how well the artist has managed to integrate textual details into the engraving!

Copper engraving from Jan Luiken, Martyr's mirror.

The Falkenstein Songs: Not Sung Here Anymore, but Still Sung on the Prairie!

Unbelievable since this happened right before our eyes:

> Hutterites from North America are coming here to visit the fortress at Falkenstein in the Weinviertel and begin to sing songs spontaneously, from memory, in really old German.

Events would be sung that their forefathers experienced almost half a millennium ago. Among the Hutterite Brethren, an entire collection of songs called the "Falkenstein Songs" have been preserved.

- The "History of the Persecution at Steinebrunn" by Antoni Erfordter, for example, has 14 stanzas.

- The Songs of Leonard Roth about the prisoners of Falkenstein – to be sung to the tune of "I Stood One Morning" – has exactly 29 verses. The song boldly reported from that night in December 1539 "Of Steinebrunn in the Gardens, of the Land of Austria," in which around 150 Anabaptists were kidnapped and brought to the fortress of Falkenstein of the family Fünfkirchen.

- In another song from Roth: "Ach Gott im höchsten Reiche" (O God in the highest kingdom) it says:

> *"O God in the highest kingdom*
> *You strong shield and buckler*
> *O Jesus Christ the same,*
> *a noble duke yet mild.*
> *O Holy Ghost with honor,*
> *Give us your divine favor,*
> *That we may together*
> *Confess you patiently."*

This song with the title *"O König Jesu Christe"* (O King Jesus Christ) was also adopted into Lutheran hymnals. It can still be found in the 1960 edition of an Austrian-Lutheran song book.

Both song writers were held captive at castle Falkenstein.

A Hutterite delegation from North America,
at the place where their forefathers lived.

Anabaptists may have been incarcerated in these newly re-discovered caves.

The Expulsion of the Hutterites

With the Battle of White Mountain in 1620, the time of Hutterites in Moravia came to an end. All non-Catholics had to leave. Many Hutterites could not resist this pressure, and, wanting to stay in southern Moravia, became part of the Catholic Church. Most likely 1/3, or 8,000 Hutterites, departed. They fled to Upper Hungary (today's Slovakia) and to Transylvania, where Hutterite settlements already existed.

By the mid-18th century only a small remnant of these Hutterites remained. They were strengthened by refugees from Carinthia in southern Austria. These were victims of a renewed wave of persecution under Maria Theresa, who deported all Protestants under her to Transylvania. These Carinthians were excited by the Hutterites faith, became baptized, and founded their own communities. They organized their communities according to the old Hutterite ordinances and shared all their possessions. This step led to a renewed wave of persecution against the Hutterites in their new home of Transylvania.

The Puzzle of Secret Underground Escape Vaults

So-called "*Earthen Stables*" can be found in Lower Austria in nearly every village. The interpretation of the purpose of them ranges from the mystical to the esoteric.

Presumably, they have something to do with the hiding of things from approaching, pillaging enemies. Some of them bear the scars of many centuries. These underground hollows are still quite puzzling.

At least for a few of them, the chronicles of the Hutterites give us a few previously unnoticed clues:

For a time, no Anabaptist sympathizers were safe anywhere. Since the Great Persecution of 1548, the Anabaptists made "*holes and pits in the ground to live in, just like foxes.*" Even at the beginning of the 17th century, Hutterites reported that their enemies, while attempting to steal their goods, "*found hidden pits and holes.*" In some villages in South Moravia, locals still speak today of so-called "Lochys" (hole-ies), referring to cellar escape systems made by the Anabaptists.

These "*secret chambers*" differ from most underground stables. They are arched and evidence the outstanding craftsmanship of miners. Many Hutterites had been Tyrolean miners. The construction is meant to confuse the intruder and to gain time to escape. Some of these vaults had proper chambers and allowed a longer stay, even with children. On the eastern shore of the March River, connecting tunnels and a ceramics repository have been found.

Such underground structures are the same in Austria, South Moravia, Bavaria, and in the Alsace, sometimes with very similar details! No wonder, since in these areas the Anabaptist movement was strongly represented and persecution was heavy there. Further research will, in the truest sense of the word, bring further understanding to "*the light of day.*"

(Mennonitisches Lexikon, Dr. Karel Cernohorsky, Brünn,
Das große Geschichtbuch der Hutterischen Brüder)

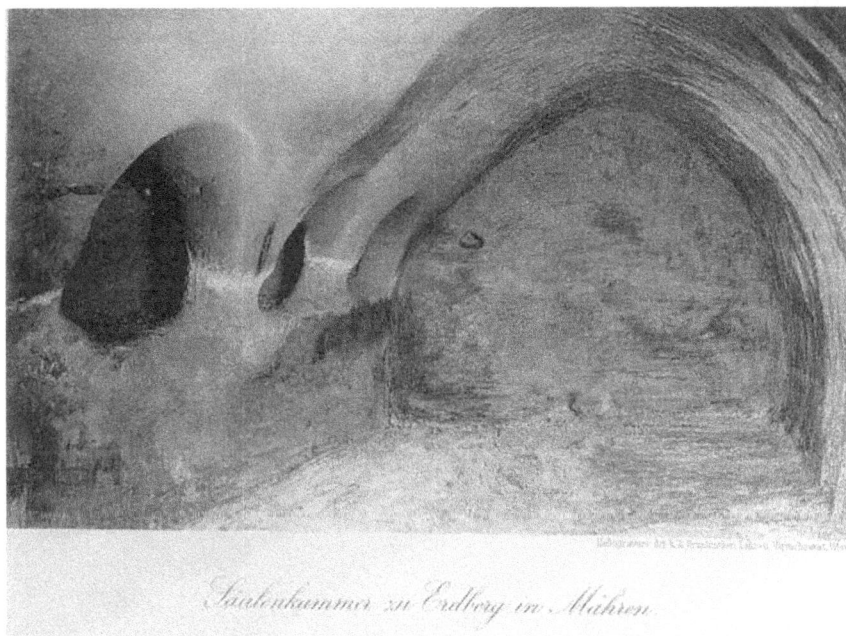

Photograph from Lambert Karner, an artifical cave from long ago, 1903

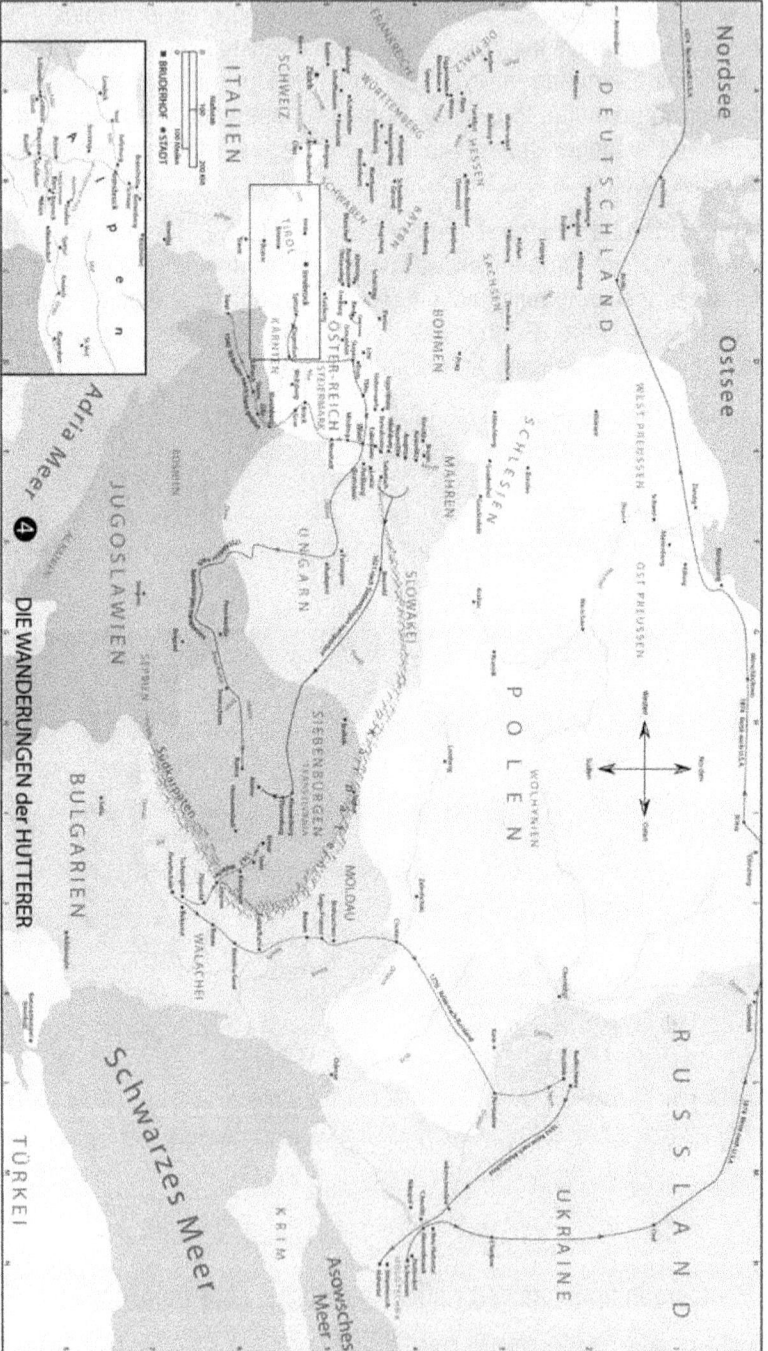

The Journeys of the Hutterites

DIE WANDERUNGEN der HUTTERER

A Matron Regulates the Faith of Her Subjects – Commission of Maria Theresa on August 8, 1778

"No new subjects shall be approved by manorial officials, nor be allowed to purchase homes without parish approval, who is not, along with his wife, a proper Catholic. Whoever shall do so shall be punished by fine or physical punishment."

"It is forbidden to speak of or discuss this religion in taverns and in the street, for which all violators will be punished."

"The foreign and domestic abusers and false teachers, Lutheran books, and transporters and sellers of them are to be stopped and held and shall be publicly displayed on the pillory, then incarcerated two years in the penitentiary. For domestic cases, if there is not improvement after punishment, each shall be deported to Transylvania. For foreign cases, after swearing an oath of eternal loyalty, the perpetrator and anyone aiding him shall be incarcerated one year and, if found to be a repeat offender, shall be deported to Transylvania." (*Knall, Dieter,* Aus der Heimat gedrängt)

Empress Maria Theresia,
oil painting by Martin van Meytens 1759.

Room F

Subsequent Groups and Spiritual Heritage of the Anabaptist Movement –

Hutterites and Free Churches Today

Once Proud Castles – Today Just Ruins!

The proud fortresses
that once bloodily persecuted the Anabaptists
are today just piles of rubble.
But what became of the children of that movement
which once rocked Europe?

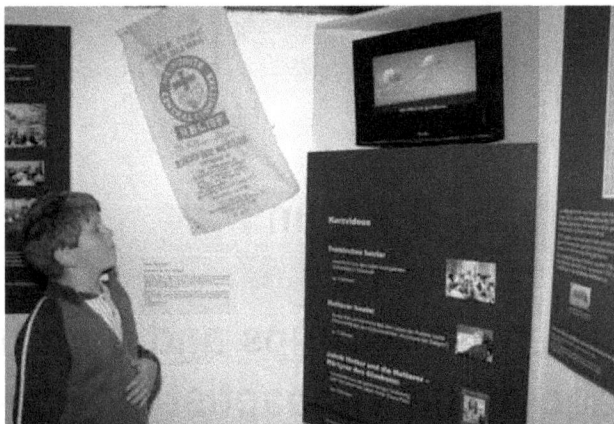

Selectable video clips show a lively perspective of the Hutterites today,
clips from a film about Jakob Hutter, as well as information about evangelical,
free churches in Austria.

Three Branches of the Anabaptist Movement Have Survived Until Today.

1. The Hutterites

The movement was founded by Jakob Hutter, born in South Tyrol, who was burned at the stake in Innsbruck in February 25, 1536.

Hutter worked as a preacher and organizer of the early Anabaptists in Western Austria. Anabaptist villages north of Vienna and into Moravia experienced the protection of protestant nobles and had nearly 20,000 members. In their common courtyards they realized the so-called "Golden Age" (1565-1578) of Christian communal living.

Older Hutterite women, Bloomfield Colony

2. The Mennonites

Founded by Menno Simons (1496-1561).

Simons was first a Catholic priest. Before his spiritual conversion he led a life of excessive gambling and drinking.

Under the influence of Anabaptist ideas he spent time in concentrated study of the Bible and the question of infant baptism:

"I examined the Scripture with diligence and accuracy, but I couldn't find any trace of infant baptism."

As a result of his study, Menno Simons founded a moderate branch of Anabaptists, who still live in the strongly peace-oriented free churches of Mennonites, who have around 1 million members worldwide.

3. The Amish

Founded by Jakob Ammann (born in 1644 in Switzerland, died before 1730).

Ammann came from the "Swiss Bretheren," known in the 17th Century as Mennonites.

In 1693, the Amish split from the Mennonites. This was due to the particular opinions and teachings of Ammann's elders on some theological issues and the strict interpretation of church discipline.

The Amish in the early 17th century lived mainly in the Alsace region of France, but faced increasing hostility and persecution. They migrated in the 18th century to Pennsylvania in North America. Today, the Amish (about 250,000 people) live in isolated agricultural areas in the United States. In many cases, they reject technical progress and accept new things only after careful consideration. Along with the other two groups, they still speak some of their old German dialect.

School Systems of the Anabaptistis and Hutterites

School desk with examples of school books in German

In every country where the Anabaptists put their feet, education was always valued. They baptized no one who hadn't journeyed the pages of holy Scripture. To the amazement of their inquisitors, these simple people, who earlier were labeled as illiterate, could always read and write. The reason for this was the education of the Anabaptists, which in its many different forms still exists among Mennonites (in Germany, Holland, North America, South America, and Switzerland) and among the Hutterite Brethren.

Religious rearing of children was always a focal point, even as it still is among Hutterites today. The **school regulations of Peter Walpot** in 1568 are still in use in their basic form.

School education begins at 2 years of age and ends at 14. The children attend the "**Klana Schual**" (small school) until age 5. After that, in North America, they continue with normal elementary education in the English language. In the Unites States, the colony chooses its own English teachers; however, in Canada, the state determines them.

Besides normal school operations, preachers on many afternoons gather the children for "**deitschn Schual**" (German school). There they receive in high German their instruction in faith and learn writing according to current German norms through which they bring their mother tongue to paper in gothic style type. (See schoolbooksin Room E!)

Further studies are the exception, as "to live requires no studies."

The ultra-practicality of this lifestyle has been often criticized. Actually, general education isn't that important to Hutterites. Nevertheless, in the area of theology and history, they have produced men of astounding quality, like Peter Walpot, Peter Riedemann, Andreas Ehrenpreis, Kaspar Braitmichel, Hauprecht Zapff, and Johannes Waldner. Their good reputation as doctors and ability to incorporate new technologies in meaningful ways shows their amazing variety of talents.

Mennonite Lexicon, Vol 4; Wolkan, Rudolf, The Hutterites; Mumelter, G., The Hutterites. Tyrolian Anabaptist Communities in North America)

The Hutterites Today – They're Still Around!

Today over 50,000 Hutterites live in the USA and Canada in large colonies of groups with up to 100 inhabitants.

The continuity of Hutterite communities from the early 16th Century until today is impressive, their history of living with property in common notwithstanding. This is an amazing phenomenon.

It should not be forgotten that, even though the Hutterites life in communal groups is fascinating, they have not been spared numerous crises and resistance over their nearly 500-year history.

The Hutterites have managed to reorganize themselves time and again. They have held to a vast collection of writings from the 16th and 17th centuries which have acted as their standard for living. These writings have also passed along their traditions over the generations.

(*Vgl. Schlachta, Astrid von*, Die Hutterer zwischen Tirol und Amerika)

A bird's eye view of Bloomfield Colony

The Hutterites Tomorrow?

The Hutterite community of the 21st century presents itself as an astoundingly stable one, though faced with many challenges.

Take the aspect of language, for example. A tyrolian-carinthian, with a dialect containing an increasing number of English words in everyday language, experiences High German in sermons and spiritual books and English as his trade language. In past years English has entered even religious life, which affects one's faith directly in some circles. The reason for this is an "English" form of religiosity which competes with the Hutterite, history-engraved sense of devotion to God. Hutterites can rely on a 500-year-old treasure chest of spiritual writings, which pass down the deep spirituality of the church and the experience of persecution, deportation, and death, and especially the experience of the fellowship of the Brethren community. This Hutterite treasure could lose its meaning, if German develops only the function of a "dead" church language, which only the spiritually elite understand.

The raising of youth and their ties to the church reveals a challenge. The rate of young Hutterites, who temporarily leave the community and then usually return, is relatively high. But these who return are people of the 21st century, too. Influences from outside find their way into the Hutterite community – technical advances in private and school life are just one aspect. In general the desire for individually stylized lives collides with the lifestyle of communal living, which isn't thoroughly fascinating for every Hutterite young person.

Young Hutterite woman at a computer, Bloomfield Colony.

The Hutterites are invited to answer questions of separation and openness to the outside world with flexibility so that they can keep their clearly Hutterite identity as well as carefully accept change. A community that has centuries old traditions as its roots runs the risk of growing stiff, if members are only surrounded by a skeleton of lifeless rules and standards.

The further history of the Hutterites will remain exciting. Coming generations will be asked to grapple with their roots and to respond accordingly. Their almost 500-year history speaks for the success of the Hutterite model, a success, which was sometimes bought with crisis and new beginnings. The flames in front of the "Goldenes Dachl" (Golden Roof), which stood at the beginning of their history, and the suffering of the ensuing persecution, couldn't strangle the living faith of the Hutterites.

(by Schlachta, Astrid, From Getzenberg to the Prairies; from the booklet "The Hutterites", Schloßbergspiele Rattenberg 2004)

What Distinguishes the Hutterites from Other Free Churches

- **Hutterites today maintain a lifestyle of common, shared wealth.**

  For other free churches, this level of community is almost unknown.

- **Hutterites hold strongly to their traditional culture (clothing, language, etc.)**

  The members of other free churches live their faith in the midst of their culture.

- **The Hutterites are thoroughly pacifistic.**

  Only in a few free churches is a thorough pacifism a central issue.

- **Most Hutterites live in a strong disassociation from society.**

  Most other free churches are often adapted to their respective societies, but desire to win them to their faith.

Voluntary Renouncement of Wealth

The Hutterites and golden necklaces

The effort to impress others has been enormous for millennia. Since the end of the Middle Ages, there were particularly large differences between the rich and poor.

The response of the Hutterites:

> The desire of Christians should be to please God and not people. "Anyone who recognizes this will henceforth forget all pearls, gold, and silk collars."

> *Riedemann, Peter*, Rechenschaft unserer Religion, um 1550.

For the Anabaptists, Christian love was to be lived out under the following motto:

> "I shall do without luxury, so that help can be provided to those who suffer lack of what is needed to live."

The equipping of all Hutterite facilities was therefore deliberately simple and modest. This was true for their farms, rooms, tools, and clothes.

One's personal property often fit in a single flour sack.

This trunk typifies the humble, personal belongings of earlier days.

Married couples often had only a small bunk in the multi-level floors of their Brethren farms. Each couple was separated from the next by only a few fabric walls!

No great treasures could be found in these berths:

- A water jug to wash

- A linen cloth to dry

- A bed pan

- A footstool on which clothes were hung

- In the best cases, a chest with only a very few personal items

The many colonies of the Hutterites have remained astonishingly self-sufficient. The production of shoes, brooms, and even the binding of books is completed by them just as much as the cutting of hair.

Handmade "Waldner" Girl's Shoes

These shoes were made by Paul Waldner in the Blumengart Community, Canada. Of note here is the common Hutterite last name of "Waldner." This typical Austrian name is found among hundreds of Hutterite families. Almost all of these 50,000 Hutterites trace their lineage back to around 15, mostly Austrian families.

Flour Instead of Revenge!

Their Support Shipments Were Welcome

With empty hands they were driven out of the Habsburg Empire 400 years ago because of their faith. People were only interested in their hard-earned money and their wealth was plundered. The last of them were so oppressed that they were forced to flee in secret.

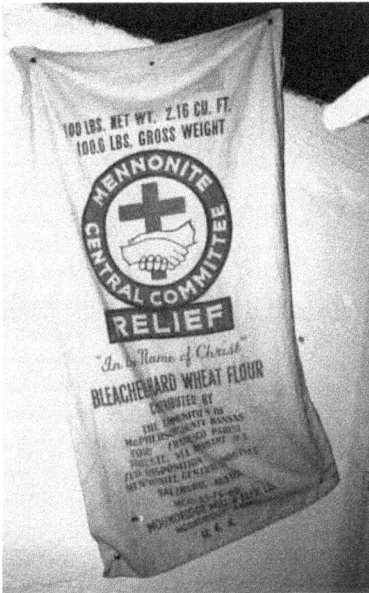

After World War II, Austria herself lay in rubble, the population was starving, and thousands had fled as refugees. Anabaptist descendants from groups of free churches didn't delay to help, like the Mennonites of North America.

They sent flour and warm blankets for the starving population. The true motive for this was clearly written on the bulging sacks:

"In the name of Christ"

Common Features of Most Free Churches: Are Free Churches Really More Free?

- **Adherence to the four pillars of the Reformatio**

  1. Jesus alone: he is the only Giver of salvation.

  2. The Bible alone: it alone is the standard for faith.

  3. Grace alone: salvation from God is an unearned gift.

  4. Faith alone: it is the only condition for receiving salvation

- **Adherence to the Apostle's Creed**

- **Adherence to the personal decision of faith and the following of Jesus Christ with one's life**

Formal affiliation with a church isn't enough. A personal commitment to Jesus Christ is needed along with a willingness to obey Him.

- **The personal decision to be baptized**

As a result, baptism follows personal faith. Pedo-baptism (infant baptism) is generally denied, since the Bible teaches that baptism always follows faith and never precedes it. Most often, those being baptized are fully immersed in water after they have publicly testified of their faith.

- **Personal decision of membership**
- **Personal decision to financially support the church**
- **The autonomy and independence of local congregations**
- **Independence from the state (separation of church and state)**

In Austria, the word of "evangelikale" (evangelical) is most commonly used to describe these churches.

The church centers of free churches are mostly inconspicious yet functional. Photo of the Evangelical Church of Vienna-Floridsdorf.

Free Churches in Austria Today

The history of free churches in Austria is at the same time very young and very old

Long before the Awakening of the 18th Century in North America and England, there were already free churches in Austria. And before missionaries from America, Germany, and Switzerland came after World War II, there were Anabaptists who had already been burned on Austrian pyres.

When one takes into consideration the beginning of the Anabaptists, which began in Zurich and soon blossomed all over Austria and southern Germany, one sees that Austria has a longer history with free churches than most countries in the world. (This fact is important to understand, since many Austrians consider the Free Church movement to simply be an imported product from the USA.)

Nevertheless it is correct to note that, because of the re-catholicization of Austria, there is no direct continuity between the Anabaptists of the early modern age and contemporary free churches, although testimonies of Anabaptist faith in Austria go back to the 16th Century in various provinces.

Since the second half of the 19th Century, free churches have been reestablished and pushed dramatically forward since the 1960's.

The return of the Anabaptists of the 16th century as a long-established, Austrian faith serves as a vital element of the development of Austrian free churches.

Free Churches Worldwide and in Austria

Main Branch of Christianity	Beginning	Members/ Attenders
Roman Catholic Church		1.143 Mill.
Ancient Oriental Churches	4./5. Cent.	26 Mill.
Byzantine-orthodox Church	1054	221 Mill.
Lutheran Church	1517	72 Mill.
Protestant / Evangelical Churches	1525	600 Mill.
Anglican Church	1534	83 Mill.
Byzantine-orthodox Church	1549	75 Mill.

In the worldwide evangelical movement, to whom many free churches belong, many principles from the Anabaptists have been handed down.

These free churches comprise today one-third of Christianity worldwide.

Church service attendance in all local, evangelical churches in Austria is, according to the newest data (2007), almost twice as high as all protestant and reformed congregations put together. (Because no comprehensive statistics or research work was available, some estimating was done.)

Church Service Attendance in the Protestant Church and Evangelical Churches in Austria

Attandance

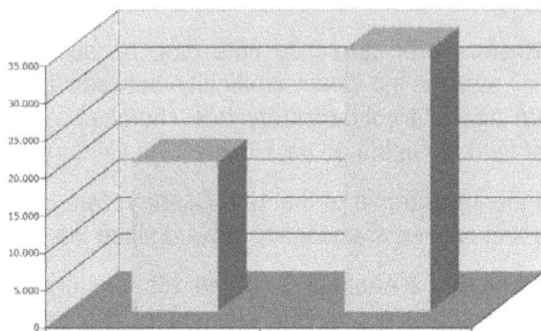

Graphic: Protestant Churches / Evangelical Churches

(See also Rathmaier, Franz, MDiv, MTh "Anabaptists, Hutterites, Free Churches Today"
Brochure from the Hutterite Exhibition at the Goldenes Dachl, Innsbruck)

Hutterites and Anabaptists: Only Martyrs and Heroes of Faith?

In the course of his conflict with Hans Hut, Hubmaier contradicted him with his own writing on freedom of faith, which he had explained in his 1524 writing titled "Of Heretics and Those Who Burn Them". He later deeply regretted this in prison.

The danger of traditionalism threatened every group. Originally, an outward-focused dynamic marked the Anabaptist movement. As time went along, however, some groups let the keeping of tradition have the upper hand. The temptation to simply rest on what earlier generations had done hindered the process of dealing with contemporary questions and problems.

A focus on one's own group of Anabaptists often restricted thinking, in that the group became self-centered instead of keeping the call to share faith with the outside world. Dogmatism and schism were the results of this, which weren't very attractive to outsiders.

Affluence with all its temptations, which had rapidly grown during the "Golden Age" of the Hutterites, didn't remain without repercussions. Only a small portion of Hutterites were ready to leave their homes for their faith after 1620.

Around the Anabaptist Museum

Outside Grounds

Chained up in One's Own House

"Electronic Fetter" for Anabaptist Women

Anabaptist women, "whose husbands were not Anabaptist, but in the right religion," were kept chained up. Under the supervision of the husband and officials, they were held prisoner in their own houses.

These women did not want to obey, like Margaret Hellwart, who insisted "on re-baptism." All conversion attempts, from church superiors to her husband, had failed miserably. Exile would also make everything worse. The household would collapse if the mother was suddenly missing. Faced with small children, the entreaties of the husbands [to the authorities] often led to capitulation. It was decided that "such a wife of a man should be kept on a chain..." This was a cheap solution, as food and security costs were covered.

Im eigenen Haus an der Kette

Eine eigenartige Praxis in der Reformationszeit.

Mehr dazu im Museum ...

Katharina Zipfel died in such a condition.
Elizabeth Reich, formally charged in 1597, was not properly connected to the chain.
Barbara Mueller was able to be, in the truest sense of the word, "let loose."

(loose translation of Kobelt-Groch, Marion, Mennonitische Geschichtsblätter)

Elisabeth Hubmaier

She was the faithful and courageous wife and companion of Dr. Balthasar Hubmaier, the leading theologian of the early Anabaptist movement. Elisabeth encouraged her husband to steadfastly endure and not to recant his faith, right up until his execution. Three days after his public execution by burning at Vienna-Erdberg, on March 10, 1528, she also was sentenced to death. Elisabeth Hubmaier was thrown from a Danube bridge with a stone around her neck. Death through drowning was the standard method of execution in those days for women heretics.

Reconstruction of a Lutheran Chapel

This Lutheran chapel from the 18th century was reconstructed according to a nearly destroyed original from Niederfellabrunn. It was brought to the Museum Village in 1997.

This building original served as a place of the celebration of the Lord's Supper and was owned by nobility. After its desecration it was used as a hunting lodge and later as a tool shed.

In the "Lutheran Chapel" visitors may view documents gathered together into a collection entitled "Protestanten im Weinviertel," compiled by Dr. Gustav Reingrabner.

The Greater Surroundings

A section of the biblical garden (herbs and other plants)

The Anabaptist Museum:
A Look behind the Scenes

How did this museum actually come about? In the summer of 2007 a special exhibition was displayed in the "Goldenes Dachel" in Innsbruck/Tyrol called "Die Hutterer – Verbrannte Visionen" (The Hutterites – Burnt Visions?) Because of its success, Karl Amesbauer initiated a number of meetings with the "Hutterites" as the main topic of discussion. As a result, Reinhold Eichinger took the initiative to found the "Hutterischer Geschichtsverein" (Society for Hutterite History). This organization, in addition to local field research, exists to bring the history of Austrian Anabaptists before the eyes of the public.

The vision was soon thereafter cast for a permanent museum. The Museumsdorf Niedersulz (located north of Vienna), along with its founder Professor Josef Geissler, offered not only an ideal atmosphere but also the necessary space for such an exhibition in the form of a period house relocated from the town of Wilfersdorf. The geographical location south of "heretic corner" in the Weinviertel/Lower Austria, right in the middle of the historical region of the Anabaptists, seemed to be the perfect place for a permanent exhibition of local Anabaptist history. Inside the museum-village there too was the thematic setting for this piece of history – a section of the village already included a Lutheran chapel, a Catholic memorial chapel, and a biblical garden. (See the map in the back of this book for details.)

From the beginning of rebuilding the relocated structure, it became clear that the planned museum would draw new groups of visitors. Even a team of Baptists from Texas (USA) was involved, volunteering manual construction labor alongside Professor Geissler. Many independent churches worldwide, including most evangelicals, see their historical roots in the Anabaptist movement. It was then no wonder that the students of the Evangelikale Akademie (Evangelical Academy) in Vienna helped to contribute to large sections of the museums displays. Astrid von Schlachta, an historian from Innsbruck, provided much-needed advice and practical support. Along with donations from the Listo family, much financial support was provided by various groups from the Bund der Evangelikalen Gemeinden in Österreich (Association of Evangelical Churches in Austria), which made the exhibited displays possible. Hutterites from North America also contributed numerous artifacts on display.

Hutterer

Geschichtsverein
Wien-Niederösterreich

Prof. Josef Geissler, founder and "soul" of the
Musuemsdorf

EVANGELIKALE **AKADEMIE**

E V A K

Ausbildung mit *Profil*

Students of the Evangelical Academy
with historian Astrid von Schlachta (foreground)

Around 1,000 guests gathered to open the museum on October 5, 2008. This was very encouraging. The Hutterischer Geschichtsverein (Society of Hutterite History) plans in the future to link various historically relevant locations together, such as the ruins of Falkenstein and the Castle of Kreuzenstein. There are already special excursions available which highlight the history of the Anabaptists in Austria.

Visitors at the opening on October 5, 2008

J. Coreth, President of the Volkskultur, Lower Austria
H. Newohradsky, second president pf the Landtag, Lower Austria
E. Röhrer, chairman of the Association of Evangelical Churches in Austria

Reinhold Eichinger and Professor Josef Geissler with VIP's from the province
of Lower Austria. Representatives of churches, mayors, historians and leaders
of the Museumsdorf attended the opening celebration.

Appendix

Museumsdorf Niedersulz

A-2224 Niedersulz 250
Tel. 02534/333
Fax 02534/333 20
e-mail:info@museumsdorf.at
http://www.museumsdorf.at/

The Museum-Village allows each visitor to dive into the history of Weinviertel villages. Tours with knowledgable guides enrich the visitor's impressions and give unexpected glimpses into the historically accurate building.

Open daily from 9:30-18:00
Last entrance: 17:00

Other opportunities:

Hutterischer Geschichtsverein (Hutterite Historical Society)

Chairperson: Reinhold Eichinger, 1210 Wien, Ispergasse 22
Tel.: 01/292 77 81, E-mail: reinhold.eichinger@gmail.com

Please take note of the comprehensive items related to Anabaptist history for sale at the gift shop. Most of the following works are available there:

Literature:

Eichinger, Reinhold – Enzenberger, Josef
Täufermuseum Niedersulz – Museumsführer, Nürnberg 2010
(German edition of this museum guide)

Holzer, Louis, Jakob Hutter und die Hutterer, Lienz 2004
Photo book of the film with the same name

Hoover, Peter, Die Feuertaufe
Das radikale Leben der Täufer – eine Provokation, Berlin 2006

Kalinova' – Fassbinder – Brückler – Brückler (Hg.),
Täufer – Hutterer – Habaner. Geschichte, Siedlungen, Keramik in Südmähren, Westslowakei und Niederösterreich, Hollabrunn 2004

von Schlachta, Astrid,
Die Hutterer zwischen Tirol und Amerika – Eine Reise durch die Jahrhunderte,
Innsbruck 2006

von Schlachta, Astrid,
Verbrannte Visionen? Erinnerungsorte der Täufer in Tirol, Innsbruck 2007

Other media:

DVD-Video:

Jakob Hutter und die Hutterer – Märtyrer des Glaubens, Taura-Film. Lienz 2004.
This historical film shows the true story of people who were most heavily persecuted for their strict pacifism and deep religious convictions.

Audio-CD:

Wenn der Glaube Feuer fängt... Lieder und Texte der Täufer,
Produzent: *Alexander Basnar,* Wien 2006

Weblinks:

www.anabaptists.eu and www.taeufer.com

Weinviertler Museumsdorf: http://www.museumsdorf.at/

Täufermuseum in Wikipedia:
http://de.wikipedia.org/wiki/Täufermuseum_Niedersulz

Wikipediaportal Täuferbewegung:
http://de.wikipedia.org/wiki/Portal:Täuferbewegung

Audiovorträge – ARGEGÖ:
http://www.evangelikal.at/155/Evangelikale/Täufergeschichte.html

Bund Evangelikaler Gemeinden, BEG: Powerpointpräsentation:
http://www.beg.or.at

Videoclip zum Täufermuseum:
http://cross.tv/videos?query=Täufermuseum&lang_switch=2

Mennonitischer Geschichtsverein:
http://www.mennonitischer-geschichtsverein.de/index.html

Hutterian Brethren Book Center:
http://www.jakobhutter.de/index.html

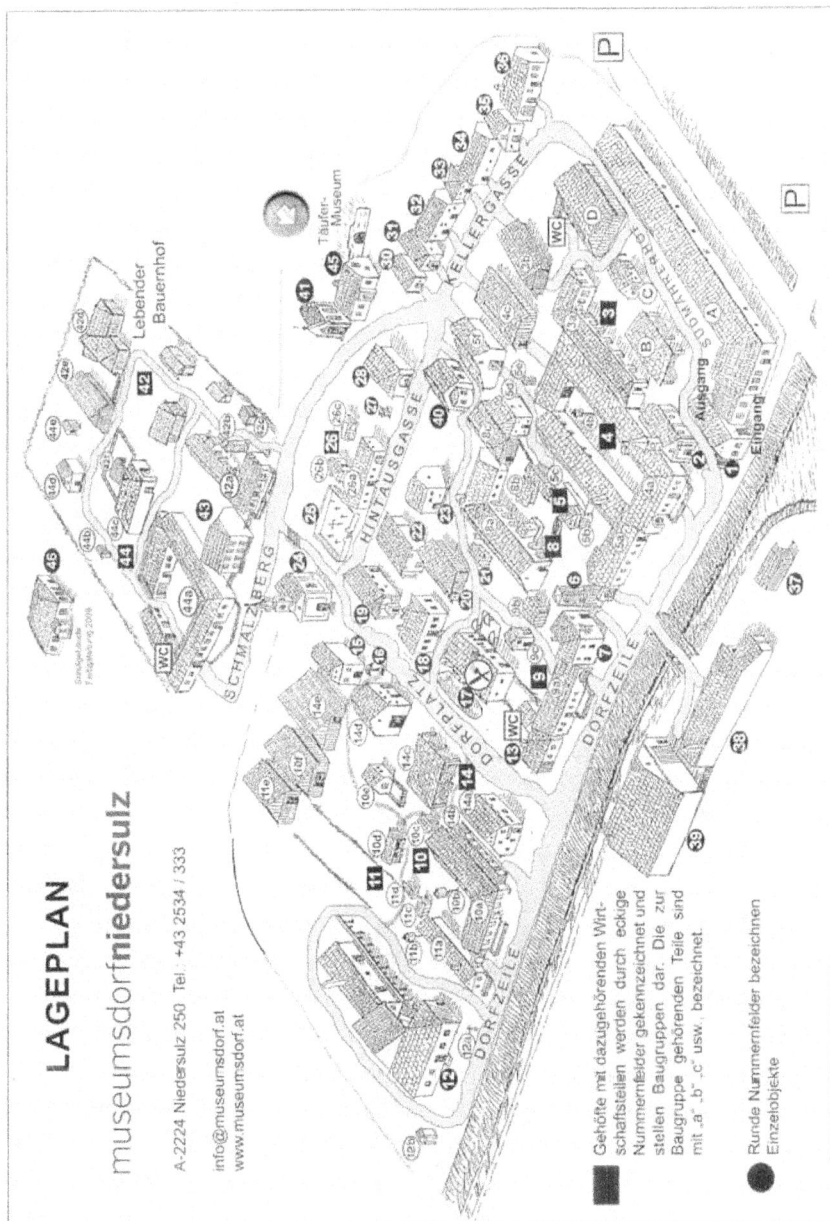

MUSEUMSDORF NIEDERSULZ

DORFZEILE:

1 Eingangsgebäude und Greißlerei · Neubau in der Art eines Weinviertler Streckhofes

2 Georgskapelle aus Obersteinabrunn

3 Hörersdorfer Hof
(Sonderausstellung: Die Wäsche ist der schönste Zier...)
3a Hakenhof aus Hörersdorf
3b Längsstadel aus Loidesthal

4 Bürgermeisterhaus
4a Doppelhakenhof aus Wildendürnbach
4b Taubenkobel · Rekonstruktion nach Vorbild aus Großschweinbarth
4c Längsstadel aus Gaubitsch

5 Drösinger Hof
5a Zwerchhof aus Drösing
5b Taubenkobel aus Walkendorf
5c Kukuruzspeicher ("Woazhäusl")
5d Presshaus und Schüttkasten aus Oltenthal · Keller
5e Bienenstand aus Niedersulz
5f Längsstadel aus Bernhardsthal
aus Spannberg

6 Schlauchturm aus Enzersfeld

7 Kleinhäuslerhaus aus Kleinhadersdorf

8 Kettlasbrunner Hof (Bauhof, kein Zutritt)
(Schusterwerkstatt)
8a Hakenhof aus Kettlasbrunn
8b Massstelg und Abort aus Walterskirchen
8c Längsstadel aus Hörersdorf

9 Sattlerhaus
9a Handwerkerhaus mit Werkstatt (Sattler)
9b Schüttkasten aus Dörfles
9c Taubenkobel aus Schönkirchen - Reyersdorf
aus Niedersulz

10 Waidendorfer Hof
10a Zwerchhof aus Waidendorf
10b Taubenkobel - Neuanfertigung in der alten Tradition
10c Mäststeig aus Großschweinbarth
10d Querschuppen - Rekonstruktion nach Vorbild aus Niederkreuzstetten
10e Ausgedingehaus aus Niedersulz
10f Längsstadel aus Großinzersdorf

11 Bad Pirawarther Hof
11a Streckhof mit Werkstatt (Knopfdrechsler) aus Bad Pirawarth
11b Taubenkobel aus Niedersulz
11c Mäststeig und Abort aus Niedersulz
11d Mäststeig aus Niedersulz
11e Längsstadel aus Obersulz

12 Hofmühle der Herrschaft Walterskirchen
12a Wegkreuz
12b Wegkapelle (Rekonstruktion aus Hohenruppersdorf)

DORFPLATZ

13 Schmiede aus Patzenthal

14 Altes Wirtshaus
14a Wirtshaus aus Poysdorf
14b Kegelbahn aus Friebritz
14c Einkehr- u. Tanzschuppen aus Hohenruppersdorf
14d Wagenremise und Schüttkasten aus Seitzersdorf-Wolfpassing
14e Längsstadel aus Waidendorf

15 Presshaus und Schüttkasten aus Herzogbirbaum

16 "Blecherner Herrgott" · Holzkreuz mit Blechkorpus (Kopie nach altem Vorbild)

17 Dorfwirtshaus - Herrschaftliches Jägerhaus aus Hohenau (täglich geöffnet)

(X) [WC]

18 Pfarrhof aus Poltenhofen

19 Kellerstöckl aus Erdpreß

20 Längsstadel aus Niedersulz

21 Bienenhütte aus Aspam/Zaya

22 Presshaus und Schüttkasten aus Wultendorf

23 Schüttkasten aus Patzmansdorf

24 Marienkapelle aus Lanzendorf

HINTAUSGASSE

25 Friedhof

26 Handwerkerhaus
26a Kleinhäuslerhaus aus Mistelbach
26b Schusterwerkstatt aus Mistelbach
26c Mäststeig aus Obersulz

27 Binderkasten (Eichenholzer)

28 Presshaus aus Niedersulz

29 Lutherische Gehteinkapelle aus Niederfella-brunn (Rekonstruktion)

KELLERGASSE

30 Presshaus aus Elbesthal

31 Presshaus aus Großinzersdorf

32 Presshaus und Schüttkasten aus Ladendorf

33 Presshaus aus Kleinschweinbarth · Keller

34 Vinothek · Presshaus und Schüttkasten aus Hütten-dorf, Kreuzkeller · (geöffnet samstags 13.30 - 18.00 Uhr, sonntags und feiertags 11.30 -18.00 Uhr)

35 Presshaus aus Drösing

36 Kleinhäuslerhaus aus Wetzelsdorf (Imkereimuseum und Fotoausstellung: Alltag im Dorf)

OBJEKTE NÖRDLICH DES SULZBACHS

37 Bienenhütte aus Oberfellabrunn

38 Kleinhäuslerhaus aus Unterstinkenbrunn

39 Kulturstadel · Längsstadel aus Zwingendorf

AM SCHMALZBERG

41 Gelöbniskapelle aus Obersulz

42 Lebender Bauernhof
42a Zwerchhof aus Prottes
42b Taubenkobel aus Bockfließ
42c Bienenhütte aus Riedenthal
42d Mäcnelfeler Kreuzstadel aus Grossenbrunn
42e Längsstadel aus Niedersulz (Gmoastodel")
42f Wagenschuppen aus Niederrußbach
42r

43 Kleinhäuslerhaus aus Altlichtenwarth (Textilausstellung)

44 Wultendorfer Hof
44a Vierseithof aus Wultendorf [WC]
44b Kukuruzspeicher aus Niedersulz
44c Längsstadel aus Pyhra
44d Presshaus aus Unterschoderlee
44e Weingartenhütte aus Niedersulz

45 Täufermuseum · Kleinhäuslerhaus aus Wilfersdorf

46 Schule aus Gaiselberg (Fertigstellung 2009)

SÜDMÄHRERHOF

A Zwerchhof (Rekonstruktion) nach Vorbild aus Neudek/Neudka (Südmähren)

B Einkehrschuppen aus Bullendorf

C Presshaus aus Niedersulz

D Längsstadel aus Velm-Götzendorf [WC]

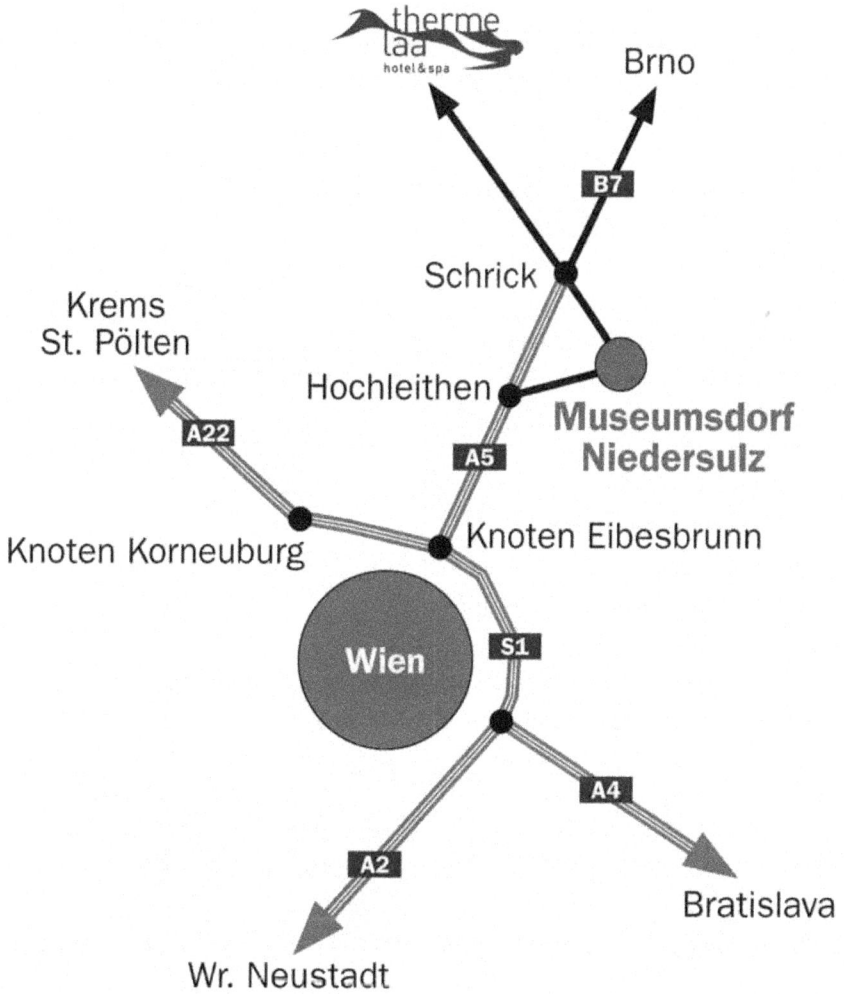

Picture Credits

Bloomfield Colony (USA): 121, 122 above, 124, 125, 126

Bund Evangelikaler Gemeinden in Österreich: 130, 139

Drews, Walter: 47, 51, 103

Eder, Hans: 43, 59, 72, 105

Eichinger, Reinhold: 11, 12, 16, 28, 32, 33, 38, 39, 56, 60, 67, 70, 76, 77, 83, 91, 98, 102, 108, 113, 120, 127, 128, 129

Evangelikale Akademie Wien: 25, 26, 27, 133, 138 below

Hannauer, Rudolf: 94

Hofer, Gerald: 116 (Starlite Colony)

Hutterischer Geschichtsverein Wien-Niederösterreich: 19, 31 above, 46, 48, 57, 79 below, 80, 81, 138 above right

Karner, Lambert: 115

Kögel, Mathis: 66, 74, 75

Kutschenmuseum Laa / Thaya: 73

Mennonitische Forschungsstelle Weierhof: 22, 62, 79 above

Museumsdorf Niedersulz: 136, 140, 145

Rathmair, Franz: 132

Schlachta, Astrid von (Sammlung von Schlachta): 64, 83 (above), 89, 100

Siebert, Mathis / Eichinger, Reinhold: 107

Taura Film / Louis Holzer: 43, 44, 45, 69, 71, 98 (middle / below), 99, 101, back cover middle, front cover above

Verlag Kellner, Korneuburg: 143, 144

VTR, Nürnberg: 7, 14, 31 below, 32, 33, 36, 122 below, 134, 135 left

All other pictures are either from the public domain or are from unknown sources.

The Hutterische Geschichtsverein (Hutterite Historical Society) has opened another exhibition in Lower Austria:

Anabaptist Chamber and Galley Ship: Burgruine Falkenstein

In remembrance of the Anabaptists of 1539, the project "From Falkenstein to the Galleys" has been completed. A depiction of the fate of those 90 men who were driven out of Falkenstein onto the galley ships is on display in the "Täufergwölb" (Anabaptist chamber). Their songs and letters can be seen in their original setting. The most current forms of media and technical production have been employed.

The **replica of a galley** ship on the castle's central grounds is designed to awaken the interests of even the youngest visitors.

Further information:
www.taeufer.net or www.anabaptists.eu or www.falkenstein.gv.at

Opening times: April to October
Saturdays, Sundays, Holidays, 10 AM to 6 PM or by appointment
E-mail: gde.falkenstein@aon.at, Telephone: +43 2554 85340
GPS: N 48.72418/ E 16.57842

This project was completed with the resources of the European Union (European Regional Development Fund), the Bundesministerium für Unterricht, Kunst und Kultur, and the Province of Lower Austria under the direction of Ing. Reinhold Eichinger in cooperation with schools and other organizations.

Informational materials for school use will be available soon.

Burgruine Falkenstein
© AustrianAviationArt.org